Finding the Life You've Been Looking For

H. NORMAN WRIGHT

HARVEST HOUSE PUBLISHERS

EUGENE, OREGON

Cover by Terry Dugan Design, Minneapolis, Minnesota

FINDING THE LIFE YOU'VE BEEN LOOKING FOR
Formerly *Simplify Your Life—and get more out of it!*
Copyright © 1998 by H. Norman Wright
Published by Harvest House Publishers, 2006
Eugene, Oregon 97402
www.harvesthousepublishers.com

Library of Congress Cataloging-in-Publication Data
Wright, H. Norman.
[Simplify your life and get more out of it!]
Finding the life you've been looking for / H. Norman Wright.
p. cm.
Originally published: Simplify your life and get more out of it! Wheaton, Ill. : Tyndale House Publishers, c1998.
Includes bibliographical references.
ISBN-13: 978-0-7369-1842-8 (pbk.)
ISBN-10: 0-7369-1842-6 (pbk.)
Product # 6918428
1. Christian life. 2. Simplicity—Religious aspects—Christianity. 3. Conduct of life.
4. Simplicity. I. Title.
BV4647.S48W75 2006
241'.4—dc22   2006001331

Printed in the United States of America

06 07 08 09 10 11 12 13 14 / VP-MS / 10 9 8 7 6 5 4 3 2 1

Contents

1

Getting the Life
You Want

"A satisfying, fulfilled life? Ha! You just don't understand my situation. Simplify my life? That's a full-time job! There's just no way for my life to ever be in balance again. I wonder if it ever was. It seems like I've been on the fast track to somewhere and nowhere ever since I was born. People had expectations of me before I even came out of the womb. And they only intensified with time. It's not just what others want now; it's what I want. What do I want out of life? I don't even know anymore, and if I did, how do I get it?"

"I'm a single parent. Sure I'd like to change my life. I suppose it's possible. If I did change, I'm afraid I'd be making a trade for what I'm doing now—surviving. I must, and I mean *must,* do what I do now in order to survive. I have two kids in school, and it's me—me who takes care of every need they have! That's a full-time job in itself. But I also have to support them. That's eight to five each day, with a half-hour commute each way. So tell me, what do I cut out to get the most out of life? This isn't the life I ever wanted. I don't think I'll ever have the life I wanted."

"I'm owned by someone else. I never planned to be, but that's way it is. My parents grew up on farms in the early 1900s. They used to tell me how hard their life was then because they had to do everything manually. They didn't have the gadgets and technology we have today. I listened to them and came to believe the more technology I owned, the better my life would be. So I've got it all. I've got a car phone, cellular phone, beeper, desktop and laptop computers. I'm tied into the Internet, and that's how I feel—tied! All this stuff isn't making my life easier. It's not giving me the life I always wanted. My life feels complicated and cluttered. Most of the time I can't even relax. But what can I do?"

Our lives are supposed to be easier, simpler, and more fulfilled. Why? Because of all the technological advances. We have gadgets to help us get organized, take control of our lives, make life more efficient—leaving us more time for doing the things we want to do. But has it worked out that way? Is life really easier and simpler? Or is it just more cluttered? Listen to a conversation between Dave and Donna as they leave on an outing.

Dave: Did you turn on the answering machine and switch the second phone line over to fax? I'm expecting some important messages, and I'm not sure whether the people will phone, fax, or e-mail.

Donna: I think everything is set. Didn't you bring your beeper? If somebody needs you right away, they can beep you or even reach you on the cellular phone. Perhaps you need to consider putting a fax in the car.

Dave: Yeah, that might make it easier. *Something* needs to make our life easier. Today was wild. I was in the middle of an important presentation, and my beeper went off. Another client needed a proposal faxed over, and can you believe it—he doesn't even own a computer! And no e-mail! The guy must be a dinosaur not to have one. And later I was taking a client to lunch, and Jenny calls me from school on her phone just when my client was getting interested in our product. And then during lunch *he* was beeped twice and got a phone call. We never finished our transaction. That's the person who is supposed to get back to me. He said he needs *my* reply immediately. Everything has to be immediate. What's the big rush? Just to cram more into our lives? What ever happened to the good ol' U.S. mail? People used to wait several days for a reply. I feel like our lives are running on the express track. How do we get off?

Donna: Is that a rhetorical question or are you really asking?

Dave: I'm really asking.

Donna: Well, I've got an answer.

Dave: You're kidding.

Donna: No, it's simple.

Dave: So tell me!

Donna: What if you turned off all the machines for several hours a day? Now wait before you say anything! Just imagine it. You look at the answering machine, and *click,* it's off. You look at your fax machine, look at the computer, e-mail, cell phone, and *click,* they're off. Now you take the rest of those technological monsters and *click! click! click!* Can you feel it? Can you feel that sense of freedom? You are your own person again. Can you feel the power and control coming back into your life?

Dave: (Silence)

Donna: Dave?

Dave: Yeah. What a feeling. But what if…

Donna: No, Dave! No buts. No what ifs. Just answer the question: Who owns you? The machines? Who's in control? Is technology making your life more fulfilled? Happier? Less stressed? If they are, keep them. If not, make some changes.

Dave, who's running your life?

That's the question we all must ask, isn't it? Who *is* running *our* lives? If you can't turn off all the machines for a day…you know what that says. Millions of people (you could be one of them) are held captive and dominated by the sounds of "time-saving gadgets" that are supposed to enhance our lives. Are you one of them? Think about the sounds of your daily life. What are they? Are they adding to your life? Who told you when to wake up? Was it really you… or the buzzer from the clock? Think of a day when you didn't hear anyone's watch or cell phone going off. We have smoke-free days and TV-free days, why not a buzzer-free day?

We jump when we hear the dryer buzzer going off telling us it's time to change loads. We jump when we hear the beep of the computer signaling yet another e-mail message. We jump when we hear the cell phone clamoring for our attention. And we jump when we hear the ding of the microwave signaling another cardboard meal. "You must! You *must* pick me up!" the machines cry out.

Why must we?

When your phone rings (especially between five and seven o'clock at night), it's usually either a computer voice trying to sell you what you don't want or an impersonal person reading a pitch to save beavers in Central America (and your donations are tax deductible!). Why do we allow ourselves to become victims to technology?

You know, you don't have to answer the phone—even if you don't have an answering machine. It's a strange thought, but it may be a beginning. To get you started, here are some suggestions to help you take control and simplify a small part of your life:

Take Control of Your Phone

1. Keep phone logs to track your phone patterns; your phone bill will give you information about your long-distance calls. Do you spend more time on the phone than you would like to spend? Consider setting a timer to limit the length of your calls.

2. Set aside time each day at home or at work to make your calls. The first thing in the morning works best for most people.

3. Develop a screening device at work and at home to screen

your calls. An answering system at home can eliminate annoying calls.

4. If you have a message system on your home phone, ask callers to let you know when they will be available for a return call.

5. Using a cell phone, portable phone, or one with a long cord enables you to accomplish other tasks while you're handling phone calls.

6. Set aside time each day to *not* take phone calls. You need the break as well as some private time. Is it really necessary to be attached to a beeper all day long? Is it really necessary to make phone calls while you're driving? It could be costly in two ways—the cost of the phone time and the risk of an accident! A *New England Journal of Medicine* article described a study indicating that driving while using a cellular phone carries nearly the same accident risk as driving while drunk.[1]

7. If you are going shopping for a specific item(s), call the store *first* to see if it's in stock.

8. Use your phone for conference calls. It beats driving.

Another important question is, Who owns you? What a strange question. I'll ask it again: *Who owns you?* A few of you might answer, "I do." I've heard some people say, "My children do. My time, my day, my night is dictated by their demands." Others say, "My spouse owns me. My schedule needs to fit within my spouse's time frame." Or maybe your career owns you. If one of these is the case for you, that's too bad. It means your life is out of balance.

Where are *you* at this point in your life? Too many of us feel that:

Life isn't fulfilling—it's out of sync.

Life isn't fulfilling—it's fragmented.

Life isn't fulfilling—it's complicated.

Life isn't fulfilling—it's stressful.

Life isn't fulfilling—it's frantic.

Life isn't fulfilling—it's overwhelming.

We honestly believe that life can no longer be fulfilling. But it can. And it's not just a dream. Balancing your life is within reach. But it means risking, changing, and taking a close look at...you. Are you ready to take back your life? To be the one who, with God, sets your priorities, schedules, and activities?

You can change your life in one of two ways: make a few revisions here and there or do a complete renovation from the inside out. We're masters at the revise-and-patch approach. Unfortunately, the patch approach to simplifying our lives simply doesn't work. In Mark 2:21, Jesus said, "And who would patch an old garment with unshrunk cloth? For the new patch shrinks and pulls away from the old cloth, leaving an even bigger hole than before." One of the initial steps in getting a balanced life is going on a radical lifestyle diet. The first step is *simplify*.

What Is a Simplified Life?

To hear how other people feel about simplifying their lives, I asked several dozen participants across the country to answer these four questions:

1. If my life were balanced, I would feel...

2. To me a fulfilled life means...

3. What keeps me from changing my life is...

4. If I were to have the life I really wanted, I would...

Throughout this book you will find 13 people's responses to these questions. But let me share some sound-bite responses with you here. Maybe you'll see yourself in them. (You may want to place a check mark by those you identify with.)

If my life were balanced, I would feel...

- lost. I love some modern things like TV, car, VCR, microwave.

- too relaxed.

- more relaxed.

- less overwhelmed, less rushed, less stress, less confused.

- relieved.

- more at peace with myself and the world.

- more at ease, more joyful, empowered with more time to develop relationships.

- as if I were forgetting something.

- at a loss for what to do next.

- unencumbered by things, more focused on our Lord, very relaxed.

- less anxious.

- less distracted from God's purpose and will for my life.

- less hurried.

- more whole and relaxed, which in turn would lead to greater joy.

- less stressed and freer to pursue things that will help me

Getting the Life You Want   13

grow in my walk with the Lord. Also, I would feel a sense
of what's important in my life.

- empty. I thrive on the many things going on in my life and
enjoy the challenge of balancing these things.

To me a fulfilled life means...
- less work and more enjoyment.

- having fewer obligations to meet but enough to keep me
busy.

- feeling as if I'm making a contribution to society with my
life.

- having fewer material belongings and fewer commitments.
Having the time to enjoy the simple pleasures of life!

- freedom from the hectic pace and pressures of today's cluttered patterns.

- knowing what is most important and living that way
without regret.

- having more time for family.

- trusting that God is in control, having fewer worries and
more joys, having fewer material things.

- having no large bills.

- feeling less stress and having more free time to enjoy life.

- being home a lot and getting enough rest. Enjoying more
family time.

- life would be dry, boring, uninvolved.

- not always feeling pressured to do things I don't necessarily
want to do.

- getting rid of the clutter—those things that rob me of
my time, including TV, household stuff that's not really

needed or just collects dust, unnecessary activities that keep me busy.

- not feeling rushed, having fewer things to care for, having time to take care of my family's needs. Everything else is extra.

What keeps me from changing my life is…
- lack of money.

- obligations.

- bills, debts.

- commitments that I've promised to fulfill. I feel too guilty to back out.

- pressure to do "God's work."

- being overwhelmed and disorganized.

- not being able to get rid of things.

- my lack of organization and motivation. I hate cleaning.

- my spouse keeps spending money.

- not knowing what to eliminate, not being able to say no, wanting to help everyone.

- needing to fix elaborate meals for my husband.

- not enough time to do what I need or want to do.

- society and trying to keep up with my kids and their activities.

- getting hung up on the expectations of the Christian community and society around me.

- attachment.

- the need to make a living.

- too much stuff and not devoting time to removing it.

- me.
- a culture that is constantly pulling me, tempting me with so many good experiences.
- peer pressure, pride of achievement.
- discipline, setting right priorities.
- not knowing what to cut out of my life.
- my inefficiency.
- paperwork, paperwork, paperwork!
- lots of kids at home, lots of places to go.

If I were to have the life I really wanted, I would...
- get rid of clutter.
- stay home more often and be involved in fewer activities.
- have a to-do list for each day, write down events in a pocket calendar when I hear about them, throw out things, get to bed earlier, pray and study God's Word daily.
- get up a little earlier so my quiet time would not be so rushed.
- reduce many of my outside activities in the evenings, be able to stay home more, have more people over to my home for encouragement.
- crawl in a closet and shut the door. Seriously, I would slow down and find out what my priorities are.
- say no more often and then wait on God's healing.
- get rid of most of the things I don't use around the house.
- seek stronger order and pray for the ability to establish priorities.
- have a smaller house, get debt free.

- give away half my stuff.

- cut back on the number of responsibilities and activities.

- cancel temptations (like catalogs), keep family activities to a minimum.

- stick to a schedule, make choices.

- cut out watching TV.

- stop trying to please others and spend more of that time pursuing a deeper relationship with God.

- enjoy life a whole lot more! Have more time to do those things with eternal value and more time to spend with my family.

- not have to work three jobs.

Did you see yourself in those responses? The "Time for Reflection" questions at the end of the chapter will give you a chance to answer the four survey questions more fully for yourself. But for now, what are your short answers to the four survey questions?

If my life were balanced, I would feel...

To me a fulfilled life means...

What keeps me from changing my life is...

If I were to have the life I really wanted, I would...

What appeals to you about bringing your lif
Maybe you're looking for more freedom or time fo
things. Perhaps you're looking to become more creative as you make
better use of your mind and imagination. What else will you gain?
What are other benefits you see in a balanced life? As you read this
book and begin to put into practice some of the suggestions, keep
in mind the benefits.

Are You Willing to Change?

If you *want* a different life, you're off to a good start. Motivation
is the first step. Finding fulfillment through simplifying your life
has to be voluntary, and you need to know why you want it. If
your family, friends, or employers are forcing it on you, it will never
happen. Don't look to them for your support. You may have to
respond "counterculture." What do I mean by that?

Simplifying your life involves readjusting your values and priorities. Be aware that your desire to change may create conflict with
other family members. They may not have any desire to change.
And if *you* change, you may throw off the established balance of
your marriage and family. Any change you make will have a direct
impact on other people. Are you prepared for this to happen? Can
you handle the resistance you'll experience? Even positive changes
you make could be met with resistance because what you're doing
creates discomfort in others, perhaps even your closest friends.
"You're not the same person you used to be" could be the com-
plaint. Others may like what you do, but resent the fact that you're
able to do it and they're not.

Understand from the beginning that simplifying your life takes
work. Don't equate *simple* with *easy*. It's like cleaning out an attic. It
takes sweat to get rid of the unused, useless, outmoded things, but

the pristine room is your reward. As you clean out your life, you'll discover treasures and even contentment and new energy.

In his book *Margin,* Dr. Richard Swenson describes some of the obstacles we may face in simplifying our lives.

> What factors make the simple life hard to obtain? If we embark on this journey, let's first decide how much of the currency of fortitude we need to bring with us. There will be tollbooths all along the route, with the costs often quite steep.
>
> No sooner have we started out the gate than we encounter our first problem: society's disrespect. If we choose to ignore fashion and status, we will not gain the admiration of our peers. From the outset, we need to decide who it is we are trying to please.
>
> To further illustrate this roadblock called social respectability, let me suggest a story and then ask a question. Suppose one day you went exploring in a cave near San Francisco. When you came out, shockingly you discovered that everyone had disappeared from the earth, transported away by invading aliens. As you search for an automobile, you find that they too have been removed. By linking your cam-recorder to a fax machine and then running both through a satellite dish, you cleverly locate the only two cars left in the United States. The first, a ten-year-old Chevrolet with ninety thousand miles, is near San Diego and could be reached in three weeks walking. The other car is the same model Chevy, only brand-new. It is on the outskirts of New York City and would require six months of walking to reach. Which would you choose?
>
> Perhaps you already suspect my point. Given this scenario, virtually all of us would be content with the older car. We would not walk an extra 161 days just for a shiny

paint job and new interior. Yet this is commonly what we do in our society—work six months for a new car instead of three weeks for a functional older one. Why do we do this? Is it because we get tired of paying for repairs? No. We buy new cars primarily for one reason: *because of the presence of other people.* We desire respectability in the eyes of others. Appearance—not function—rules us.

Continuing down the narrow road of the simple life, we keep encountering another problem: our expectations. After decades of convenience and affluence, we not only desire but *expect* ease and satiation. Gratification of our appetites has become a widespread goal not seriously challenged by the church. If we do not reprogram such expectations, we will experience recurrent frustration in our search for simplicity.

Our lack of discipline presents us with yet another obstacle. We have not needed much discipline during this era of abundance, and we have lost interest in it as a component of lifestyle. Most of us have grown soft. But the simple life is not easy, and discipline is necessary.

Finally, our own mistaken opinions of how things ought to be also trip us repeatedly. Theological confusion has permitted us first to look at what we want and then to build a theology that justifies it. For example, very little money is needed to live a fully God-honoring life. Yet somehow we have incorporated money into our theological construct. True enough, we need a lot of income to live as our society does, to partake in the many benefits of our age. But it is not true that we need a lot to live on.[2]

How Will You Change?

If you have decided that you want a balanced life—a new

approach—simplify is the first step. If you want to simplify your pace, your expectations, your activities, your possessions, your relationships, and your ministry life, then this book will help. It will ask you many questions to help you understand what is really important to you, what matters, what you value. It will also suggest many things to try as you prune things you decide do not belong in your life.

Yes, it is uncomfortable to take stock of your life and make changes, but it's also exciting to realize that you *can* change, that you *can* make your life more manageable. Remember that simplifying your life is not a onetime process. It's an ongoing pattern of life. We need to keep asking ourselves questions such as, "Why am I doing this?" and "Why am I doing it this way?"

In my home and office I have a paper shredder. It has a purpose. It's used for the unnecessary, the antiquated, the private files that need to be discarded so that no one can use them again. Such is the task of simplifying our lives. Simplifying can mean getting rid of something permanently rather than simply shifting it around and stacking it differently.

What Approach Will Work for You?

Some of you have decided that you need to simplify your lives, but you are discouraged because your previous attempts have led to discouraging results. Most of us have had that experience. But don't let that keep you from trying again! Try a different approach this time. Each of you will simplify in a way that is unique to your own style and temperament.

Stephen Covey, Roger Merrill, and Rebecca Merrill describe several organizational approaches in their book *First Things First*. One or more of these approaches may be valuable to you. As you read about these approaches, ask yourself, "Would this work for me? Would I *want* to do it? Do I *need* to do it?"

1. *"Let's get organized!"* Many books and management trainers tell us that we need to evict the chaos from our lives. Just get organized! If we can't find what we want when we want it, the solution is organization. The answer to simplifying our lives is some type of organizational system. The message is: You need to organize your life. You need to organize the *things* in your life. Do you have a place for your car keys, glasses, pens? Are the kitchen cupboards organized? You need to organize the *tasks* in your life, making a to-do list for each day, week, month and year. You need to organize *people*. Give them your requests in writing; give them tasks they're capable of doing; develop a system of follow-up with them.

The upside of this approach is that organization does save time and can lead to increased efficiency. There's no doubt about that….The downside of this approach is that it can become so consuming for some people that organization *becomes* the goal rather than allowing organization to *serve* the goal. It's possible to spend more time getting ready to do something than getting it done.

2. *The survival approach.* In the survival approach to organization, people protect their time so that they can use it to do what they need to do. Sometimes we end up feeling that everyone else owns a piece of us, and we're torn in so many directions. We're interrupted by the phone, other workers, the children, and even the pets. If your personality preference is introversion, these interruptions are especially disruptive and draining.

The survival approach helps us defend ourselves so we can accomplish and simplify. How? Three ways are available: insulation, isolation and delegation.

First, some people insulate themselves by using others to interact for them. People do this in their offices and in their homes. I've seen ten-year-old children who were taught to screen all their parents' calls.

Second, others isolate by making themselves totally unavailable to a person or machine. People put "Do Not Disturb" signs on their doors, or they don't answer the phone.

Third, some people delegate their work to qualified people.

The upside of this approach is that it sometimes allows people to get more done, sometimes in a more efficient way. The downside is that life can't be lived in isolation. If we withdraw from others, relationships can deteriorate.

3. *Set goals.* Countless books describe how we can set immediate, short-term, mid-term and long-term goals. Goals can motivate and lead us forward. They help us catch a vision of what we want to accomplish. A goal can function like a magnet that draws us forward.

The upside to this approach is that those who are committed to it and know how to set goals usually accomplish them. Goals give direction. The downside is also a reality. Sometimes people blindly adhere to achieving a certain goal, only to discover that achieving it didn't satisfy. Sometimes the price of achieving a goal is too high. And sometimes people pursue their goal so relentlessly that they fail to enjoy themselves on the journey.

4. *First things first.* Prioritizing is a very useful approach for many people. It's a matter of focusing time, attention and energy on the most important tasks first. According to this approach, doing first things first will help people feel more fulfilled and satisfied.

The upside of this approach is that it gives a sense of order to what we do. Focusing on values and beliefs helps put the most important things first. Clarifying values gives the structure needed to determine what to do first. The downside to this approach is that because many people haven't thought through their values and beliefs, they find it hard to figure out what is the most important thing to do first. Their priorities can fluctuate.

5. *The magic tool.* You've seen the pitches for these tools. If you have the "right" portable-computer watch, the right planner, the right calendar, the right laptop, the right cell phone you'll have more time, organization, and simplicity in your life. This approach uses technology or system tools to gain control.

The upside of this approach is that tools do help us to remember all of our appointments, birthdays, trips, responsibilities. They can help us organize our priorities and goals. The downside is that the tools can become obsessions. I've seen some people who collect every planning system and gadget imaginable. A tool works if you use it. But many tools only gather dust, generate guilt from their lack of use, and add to the clutter.

6. *The "master your time" approach.* This is a skill approach aimed at learning to master your time. This can be done by

incorporating many of the other approaches, such as setting goals, prioritizing to-do lists, and using a planner or calendar.

The upside of this approach is it can be helpful just to become more aware of the time crunch in your life. The downside is time management can be a superficial solution. Most time-management approaches are heavy on technique and weak on getting to the core issues for the struggle with time.

7. *Go with the flow.* This approach says that if we go with the flow of life, we'll find balance and discover a simpler lifestyle. It advocates a more relaxed perspective of getting things done. If it happens, it happens.

The upside of this approach is that it steers people away from their urgency addiction. The downside is that it seems quite nebulous and aimless. It's a drifting-with-the-tide approach and does not seem to have any vision, purpose or balance.[3]

What will work for you? Keep an open mind, evaluate, implement, and then evaluate once again.

Where Do We Go from Here?

In the remaining chapters of this book we will explore six areas that may need changing in your life. These are steps involved in getting the life you've always wanted.

1. *Pace:* We need to slow our pace so that we can catch our breath and take charge of time rather than have it take charge of us.

2. *Expectations:* We need to pare down the expectations others place on us, and we need to examine our expectations of ourselves, life, and others.

3. *Activities:* We need to ask ourselves why we do what we do so that we can reduce our activities to the things that matter most.

4. *Possessions:* We need to declutter our things and our need for things by learning to live with less.

5. *Relationships:* We need to simplify our relationships so that we are not drained either by people who clutter our lives or emotional baggage that we need to toss out.

6. *Ministry lives:* We need to make sure we are involved in ministry activities that not only match our gifts and abilities but also are those to which God, not society, calls us.

The final chapter will help you review what you have learned and help you set up a plan that will work for you—with your individual needs, your individual style, your individual life situation, and your individual beliefs and values. Attaining the life you've always wanted is a process.

I'm excited about what our lives can be like if we ask ourselves some important questions, take some small steps in a positive direction, free ourselves from the things that keep us in the rat race. Remember, you *can* have the life you've always wanted!

Time for Reflection

1. Write several paragraphs to flesh out your responses to the four questions from the nationwide survey.

   • If my life were balanced, I would feel…

   • To me a fulfilled life means…

   • What keeps me from changing my life is…

   • If I were to have the life I really wanted, I would…

   You may also want your family members to respond to these questions. Then you can discuss them together.

2. What will be the greatest payoff for you if you change your life?

3. What organizational approaches have you tried? Have they helped or hindered you?

4. Which of the five areas (pace, expectations, activities, possessions, relationships) are you most excited about working on? Is this the area that needs the most work in your life?

One Person's
Reflections on Life

- *If my life were balanced, I would feel…*more confident in the workplace, school, and family. I would feel less rushed to do things that people rely on me to do. I would reduce negative thoughts and appreciate and accentuate the positive things about life. I would listen more, especially to God. I would also have a better sense of time.

- *To me a fulfilled life means…*having my priorities in the right order and having a balance in my values, morals, and integrity.

- *What keeps me from changing my life is…*no surprise—it's me! That's it. I can't blame something or someone else. I sometimes am too proud to admit that I need help. I often am not humble enough to learn how to strengthen my life, especially my spiritual life.

- *If I were to have the life I really wanted, I would…*need to seriously reduce my stress. I would make time to do the essentials. I would stop judging others because I realize that I do the same things they do. I would hold true to my values and my sense of worth. I wouldn't procrastinate. And I would develop a better sense of time.

2

Time—Friend or Foe?

"I'd just like to pass the time away."

"I just can't afford to waste my time."

"Soon my time restraints will be lifted, and I'll…"

"Someday, when I get time, I'm going to…"

Common phrases. Well-intended phrases meant to correct, simplify, streamline, and bring balance into life. Phrases designed to ease out tension and give us hope. But they're phrases that all too often remain empty dreams.

How do you "get time" or "find time" or "restrain time" or "waste time"? Have you ever thought about some of the phrases we use when we talk about how we use time? We stretch it (I didn't know it was elastic!). We juggle it (does time come in balls, hoops, or pins?). And we schedule it (do we use a timer for time?).

In fact, how do you even define the word *time?* How do you explain it? Did you ever stop to wonder whether Adam and Eve had a sense of time? Did they have some sort of clock to mark the passing of the hours? Probably not.

The first clocks were introduced during the 1200s and were some kind of alarm. In the 1300s the dial and hour hand were added. By the 1600s the minute and second hands were in evidence.[1] Look at some of the gift catalogs today or go into a department store. You'll be amazed at the variation and sophistication of some of the "time-saving" timepieces available today. Yes, clocks have been around for centuries. So has the frustration with time constraints. People complained about the sundial in 200 BC! Plautus wrote: "The gods confound the man who first found out how to distinguish hours! Confound him, too, who in this place set up a sundial, to cut and hack my days so wretchedly into small portions."[2]

Everything is lived according to the clock, by now so accurate that we can measure the speed of subatomic particles. We wear time like manacles on our wrists and move to its inexorable beat. Time is what we use to measure our lives: a second, a minute, an hour, a year, a decade, a lifetime. All of us depend on clocks because we have become slaves to time.[3]

Is your life dominated by the clock? Does your watch tell you when to start work, when to play, when to eat or sleep? Do you ever say "It's too early to go to sleep" or "It's not yet time for dinner" or "It's too late to nap" or "It's too late to have a snack"? If you do, you need to ask: "Who's in control of my life?" Is it you or your clock?

The more refined our time-saving methods have become, the greater our struggle with time. Time is supposed to be our servant, not our master.

Controlling Your Time

One of the elements of a balanced—a fulfilled—life is being able to control time. But is that possible? How often have you thought or said, "Just as soon as such and such happens, I'm going to have more time"? I know people who've been saying that for the past 20 years. But it never seems to happen. Isn't it interesting how we use the phrase "I don't have time" to decline invitations or to avoid taking on another responsibility? Have you ever kept track of how often you think or say this? The reality is, we *do* have time. It's just that we value doing something else instead—and we *choose* to do the something else.

Time Robbers

You're probably being robbed each day, and you may not be aware of it. Who's the thief? The time bandit. How does he operate? In many ways. He shackles you to your clock. He misplaces your car keys, creates interruptions, double-books activities, and makes you forget that you already have too many activities for that day. The bandit steals not only your time but also your energy. He does this by convincing you to buy into outmoded beliefs, rules, shoulds, and myths. His greatest delight is to see you spin your wheels and lose your joy, spontaneity, satisfaction, creativity, and productivity.[4]

In his Time and Life Management seminars, Hyrum Smith asks participants to identify the biggest time robbers in their lives. Participants learned that most of their top time robbers were imposed on them by other people; the other time robbers were self-inflicted. What are the time thieves in your life? Unless you identify them, they will continue to pick your pocket. Perhaps you'll recognize these.

1. *Interruptions.* You know what interruptions are, especially if you have children. The interruption could be a phone call, someone at the door, a business associate who comes to your office and says, "This will only take a minute." (If I'm busy and really don't have a minute, I usually start counting aloud: "59, 58, 57…" This person soon gets the hint.)

Some interruptions are necessary, but most are unnecessary. Sometimes we interrupt ourselves by allowing ourselves to be distracted or even by creating a distraction. Some people are wired this way, and they love the variety that interruptions bring. To them interruptions are merely possibilities. Extroverts are energized by interactions with others. They enjoy socializing and look for any opportunity to do so. If they don't enjoy what they're doing, they look for any excuse to break away from it.[5]

Think about the interruptions in your life. Do they control you, or do you control them?

Why do we allow interruptions to occur? First, we assume that every interruption is legitimate. It's a "necessary" interruption, or so we think. And when we interrupt what we're doing, we send a message to the people who interrupt us. By default we're telling them that whatever they interrupt us for is more important than what we were doing. We only reinforce their tendency to interrupt us again!

Second, we allow interruptions because we assume that if we don't, we'll offend other people. We're afraid to do that, so we give in.

Third, we may also allow interruptions because we don't want to be left out of anything. We want to know about everything that is going on. We may allow the events around us, which include interruptions, to feed our sense of importance. Our ego gets involved.

How do you feel when you're interrupted? How do interruptions contribute to the clutter in your life? You may not be able to control whether or not you're interrupted, but you can control how you handle it when you are. If you're able to say "This isn't a good time, but I could talk in an hour" or "I can give you two minutes now and perhaps more later," you've taken an important first step.

2. *Procrastination.* Procrastination is a time robber we inflict on ourselves. Nobody else does it for us. It usually comes in two forms: conscious and unconscious. Sometimes we consciously procrastinate; we know what we're doing. Other times our procrastination is unconscious; we're not even aware it's happening. Whether your procrastination is conscious or unconscious, it contributes to chaos in your life. You lose opportunities. You are forever playing catch-up. You have to generate excuses. And you're seen as unreliable.

Why do we put things off? We don't like doing unpleasant things. When we have to do anything that requires leaving our comfort zone, we'd rather not. We procrastinate because our lives are so disorganized that a task is buried and forgotten. But for the overworked, over-committed man or woman, procrastination seems to become a by-product of overcommitment. We set ourselves up to procrastinate.[6]

For help in doing the things you don't like to do, try this method.

How to Do What You Don't Like to Do

A. On two sheets of paper—one for tasks at work, one for tasks at home—make two lists of things you don't like to do. Make the lists as long as possible.

B. Across the top of each sheet, write these four categories: Reason, Solution 1, Solution 2, How I would feel if I did it.

C. For each task that you listed, write down why you don't complete the task. (It could be you just don't like to do it, you can't see any sense in doing it, fear of the unknown, fear of failure, you don't know how, it won't help, it takes too much time).

D. Next write down two solutions for getting the task done. (List creative options like bribing your kids to do it, hiring a college student, doing a trade-off with a friend, asking someone at church who knows how.)

E. Then write down how you will feel when it's done. Doing this has motivated some people to get with the program and complete what they've been putting off for years. Anyway, it's worth a try![7]

3. *Perfectionism.* Perfectionists can be consummate procrastinators. They don't want any performance on their part to be less than complete and flawless. If what they do isn't perfect, perfectionists feel as if they are not valuable, capable, or worthwhile. Their standards for success are so high that their thoughts and feelings cripple their efforts. Because they're afraid to fail, their minds create worst-case scenarios. They become preoccupied with their own deficiencies and create nightmare visions of what might happen. "Don't even attempt it" is their motto.

Perfectionists wait for the perfect moment, the perfect conditions, the perfect opportunity, none of which ever comes. Underlying this problem is the perfectionists' urge to prove their worth by accomplishing, achieving, or producing things perfectly. No wonder procrastination becomes part of their lives.[8]

4. *Backlogs.* Time thieves also steal through backlogs, the lists of items that weren't done, need to be done, and will get done... sometime. There's only one problem. When we work from behind,

from a catch-up position, we never really catch up enough to go back and catch up! Backlogs will control us.

But there is hope. If backlogs are part of your life, commit yourself to two things: getting caught up and living by a "frontlog." First, make a list of things you need to do to get rid of the backlog. Evaluate the list. Does everything need to be done? What things can you delegate? Then make a list of things you can do to eliminate the backlog. Second, determine to live by a frontlog. Anticipate things that need to be done in the future. Then make a list of those things, and start to chip away at the list so that you're always one step ahead of yourself.

I've done this with my writing for years, but I didn't realize that's what I've been doing. I set a three- to four-month schedule for writing a book. I know how many words I need to produce each day and each week in order to finish on time. Within a month I usually find that I'm ahead of my schedule. It's a good feeling because I know that if I hit an off-week, I won't really fall behind.

5. *Shifting priorities.* Another time thief is failure to hold to our priorities. We allow immediate needs to dictate what we will do. Whatever's urgent at a specific moment gets the attention. For some people this happens weekly, daily, or even hourly. It can occur anywhere—at work, at home, while out shopping. Many men and women become addicted to the adrenaline rush of it. If you find yourself shifting priorities too often, stop and ask yourself what is happening. Are you allowing the urgency of the moment to dictate your priorities? What will happen to your other priorities if you give your attention to the immediate "crisis"?

6. *Failure to plan.* Planning is essential for getting the most out of life. Poor planning robs you and others. Planning usually

includes having a goal or a vision. Scripture reminds us of the importance of having vision: "Where there is no vision, the people perish" (Proverbs 29:18 KJV). But vision and planning need to be coupled with God's wisdom and leading. "We can make our plans, but the LORD determines our steps" (Proverbs 16:9).

Planning helps us move from the present to the future. Your vision in reading this book may be to discover the life you've always wanted. That's good, but unless you take the next step, nothing may change. Intentions without a plan usually lead nowhere.

Sometimes you have so much to do and so many things coming at you that you feel as if you don't have time to plan. That was the response of 72 percent of the participants in a national survey shared in Alec Mackenzie's book *The Time Trap*. My response to that is similar to what I say to the counselee who says he or she is too busy to read any of the assigned homework: "How much time do you spend watching TV, talking on the phone, or fretting about what needs to be done?" That usually does the job. We choose what we value. You can drift through a day, or you can move through the day with purpose. To be blunt, the excuse (not the reason) "I don't have time" isn't valid. The statement "I'm choosing not to spend time planning because other things are more important to me" is more accurate as well as honest.

Try this. Take two or three minutes and list what you have to do. Then prioritize each item on a scale of 1 to 5, with 5 being the most important. Take one 5 item and list three things that you will do to accomplish it. Now you're on your way!

However, remember that even when you plan, you need some flexibility because plans do change. Locking yourself into a dead-end approach would be as detrimental as having no goal or plan at all. [9] This fact is stated in an ancient book: "It is pleasant to see plans develop. That is why fools refuse to give them up even when they are wrong" (Proverbs 13:19 TLB).

As you read this, some of you may be muttering, "I find planning restrictive, confining, and limiting. If I plan too much, I might miss out on something else." Some of you are wired in ways that war against planning. Your personality preference is to wing it through life. You accomplish things, but usually in last-minute spurts. Winging it works for you, but your style may not work for your family members or coworkers. If you resist planning, give it a second look. Make sure you're not avoiding it just because it's unpleasant for you.

7. *Television.* This time stealer may surprise you. But before you skip this paragraph and move on to something that you think relates to you, hear me out. If you're an average American, you have 12 months available to you during the next year. That's not really profound, is it? But *this* fact (not supposition) may shock you. Over the next year, the average American will spend the equivalent of 2 months watching the tube! In fact, if you're like most Americans, by the time you reach the age of 72, you will have spent *12 years* of your life watching television. Is that really what you want for your life? Half of Americans admit to watching too much television. They know it's a problem. And then they complain about not having enough time! Most children begin watching television before they can talk. By the time many children are 6 years old, they will have spent more time watching television than they will spend speaking with their dad during their entire lifetimes. For many people, television is an addictive drug. Fifty to 60 percent of children between the ages of 6 and 17 have television sets in their rooms, and 70 percent of daycare centers use televisions to entertain (and babysit) the children. Is that what you really want?[10]

Entertainment is supposed to be just that—entertainment—not a controlling force in our lives. Neil Postman, the author of *Amusing Ourselves to Death,* has shown that entertainment has become the dominant force of public discourse in our society. It affects the arts, sciences, politics, education, and religion. Feasting on television can sap your time and energy as well as make your everyday life seem a bit drab by comparison. Life on television is supposed to be superior to reality, and with the event of virtual reality, we are faced with something that will become a dangerous narcotic if it is not controlled.[11]

If you spend more time in front of the television than you would like to admit, ask yourself these questions:

- Who's in the control booth when it comes to the use of my time and my television viewing?

- How does the following verse speak to my family's television involvement? "Don't copy the behavior and customs of this world, but let God transform you into a new person by changing the way you think. Then you will know what God wants you to do, and you will know how good and pleasing and perfect his will really is" (Romans 12:2).

- When I am 72, do I want to look back and say, "I spent 12 years—one-sixth—of my life watching television"?

Making Wise Use of Time

Are you interested in a look at how you possibly will spend your time in the future? Time analysts are now able to tell in advance how we make use of the time allotted to us. I wonder what we would do differently if we knew at an early age that we would spend 1,086 days "sick." The average person does. And you know as well as I do that some of our illnesses are preventable. Do you want to spend 1,086 days sick? Not likely.

You may be surprised to discover that you will spend eight months of your life opening junk mail. Do you want to spend two years of your life on the telephone? Do you want to spend five years waiting in line or nine months waiting in traffic?

Just the basic necessities of life consume a large quantity of time. You'll spend four years cooking and eating. (You can't live on McDonald's, Burger King, and Taco Bell all the time. If you do, you may have part of the reason for those 1,086 sick days.) You'll spend a year-and-a-half dressing, a year-and-a-half grooming, and (get this) seven years in the bathroom. Finally, the time experts tell us we'll spend twenty-four years sleeping and three years shopping.[12]

I don't know if all these calculations are accurate, but even if they are close we need to ask whether this is the way we want to use our time.

Years ago someone wrote an article with this attention-getting title: "If You Are 35, You Have 500 Days to Live." Your first reaction might be, "Wait a minute, that couldn't be true!" Consider what the author said though. When you take away all the time spent sleeping, working, doing odd chores, taking care of personal hygiene, taking care of personal matters, eating, and traveling— you end up with only 500 days in the next 36 years to spend as you want. Isn't that sobering? It sheds new light on what the psalmist said, "Teach us to make the most of our time, so that we may grow in wisdom" (Psalm 90:12).

Author Tim Hansel raises the question of what you would do if you received a phone call from your bank every day telling you that your account had been credited with 86,400 pennies ($864) and that the money had to be spent that day. Nothing could be carried over to the next day and when midnight hit, what you had left would be cancelled out. Would you let any money remain? It's doubtful. You would make sure every bit was used.[13]

In the book *It's About Time,* Leslie Flynn says that you and I have such a bank. It's called the First World Bank of Time. Each morning the bank credits your account with 86,400 seconds. That's the same as 1,440 minutes or 24 hours. It's the same for each one of us. And keep in mind that no balance is carried over to the next day. If you choose not to use it, you lose it. You can't accumulate it.[14]

How will you make wise use of your time? How will you take the investment God gives you and use it with purpose and meaning? Michel Quoist's prayer poem about time gives us some things to think about:

> I went out, Lord,
>> men were coming and going,
>> walking and running.
> In spite of all their grand efforts,
>> they were still short of time.
>> Lord, you must have made a mistake in your calculation.
> Lord, I have time.
> I have plenty of time, all the time that you give me,
>> the years of my life,
>>> the days of my years,
>>>> the hours of my days.
> Mine to fill up quietly, calmly.
> Up to the brim.[15]

Timetable Time and Event Time

The New Testament uses two different words for time: *chronos* and *kairos.* Time governed by the clock is *chronos;* time measured by events or special moments is *kairos*. *Chronos* could include time-tables and prearranged work schedules. Does most of your time fall into this category? *Kairos* is where life is experienced in the events—the special moments—of past, present, and future. Some people experience this rarely; other people never experience it. Their lives are ruled by the clock. These people will take their 500 days and govern them rigidly. But life is fuller when you occasionally overrule the clock and live in the special moments.

Today, in areas of Africa and in Papua, New Guinea, the concept of time as *we* understand it does not exist. In many languages there are no equivalent words for "hour," "minute," or "second." It is day when the sun comes up, night when it sets. The seasons are measured by the way crops grow or wither. And no one knows how old his parents were when they died—only that they *were* old, and dying was an inevitable and blessed event.[16]

Scripture charges us to redeem time, to use it for all it's worth: "See then that you walk circumspectly, not as fools but as wise, redeeming the time, because the days are evil" (Ephesians 5:15-16 NKJV). How are you going to redeem the time the Lord has given you?

As I'm writing this book, I am in my sixties. I don't have 500 days left. I'm not sure how many I have, but I do know the type of time I'm more interested in experiencing. The writing of this book has made that clear. And it's not just a matter of emphasizing one to the exclusion of the other. I still need my timetables, my goals, my structure, but the more flexible I am, the more the significant events can be a part of my timetable approach. I teach at conferences and seminars, usually on a time schedule. What makes these times fulfilling and memorable are the special moments with friends or an unplanned detour with my wife to see something new. The relaxation gained from the special moments make the structured timetable events worth the time and energy depletion. Blending or integrating the timetable time and events time brings a rhythm into our lives, a rhythm that God says is good for us.[17]

How Do You Use Your Time?

What about you? How do you use your time? For yourself? for others? for work? We need to keep a balance. Perhaps it's time for you to consider where it's being used. Which of the three bar graphs best describes your time use?

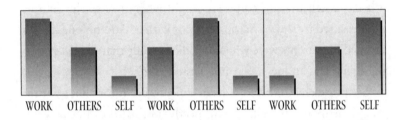

WORK   OTHERS   SELF   WORK   OTHERS   SELF   WORK   OTHERS   SELF

Where are you now? What do you want your graph to look like? Take a piece of paper and plot it out. You can redraw each of the three sections to determine your balance. What will you need to do to get it there?

The familiar story of Mary and Martha teaches us some important lessons about spending time wisely.

As Jesus and the disciples continued on their way to Jerusalem, they came to a village where a woman named Martha welcomed them into her home. Her sister, Mary, sat at the Lord's feet, listening to what he taught. But Martha was worrying over the big dinner she was preparing. She came to Jesus and said, "Lord, doesn't it seem unfair to you that my sister just sits here while I do all the work? Tell her to come and help me."

But the Lord said to her, "My dear Martha, you are so upset over all these details! There is really only one thing worth being concerned about. Mary has discovered it—and I won't take it away from her" (Luke 10:38-42).

One woman sat at his feet listening, and the other went to the kitchen to prepare the meal. Ken Gire, in his insightful books *Intimate Moments with the Savior* and *Windows of the Soul,* raises some questions about this story and about our lives. Why does Jesus take the time to stop at this house as he made his way to Jerusalem? Is he hungry, and if so, for what? Is it for food or something that the crowds or even the disciples can't give him at this time? Jesus is on his way to his death. Perhaps he's hungry for someone to minister to him, to listen to him, and to attend to him. Perhaps Martha sees only the hunger for food and the need to stay on schedule for the meals. Mary sits to listen and attend.

At times we are like Mary and Martha, torn between *chronos* (the schedule and the tasks) and *kairos* (the special moment or experience). Martha was torn between the interaction with her guest and the meal preparations. The preparations won. Mary is torn between the interaction with Jesus and the meal preparations. The interaction won. What each woman did is probably a window into her lifestyle and personality. It could be that both Mary and Martha were out of balance with their choices as to what was important to them.

But when Martha complained to Jesus, he met her fretting with a gentle response. He said that at that moment interacting with him *was* more important. Jesus corrected Martha not because of her work but because of her worry. He questioned her not because of her activity but because it dominated her.

Perhaps you've been in a similar situation. You're having guests over for an event. You want the house to be spotless, so you spend your energy on getting it clean. After all, isn't everyone going to notice? You begin the meal preparations early in the morning, snapping out orders to everyone else. The guests arrive, but after you greet them, you head for the kitchen while everyone else chats. Then you serve the meal and what took hours to prepare is consumed in half an hour. After you clean up the table, you appear in the family room just as the conversation is winding down. People are getting sleepy, and then they leave. What did *you* remember about this get-together? The fellowship or the food? The preparations or the process of interacting with each person? Was it a special occasion or another time of creating a perfect house and meal?

Do you miss out on life experiences? Does the activity, the task, the meal preparation become more important than the people you're preparing it for? It's something to consider.[18]

Time for Reflection

1. What are the typical statements you make about time? What effect do these statements have on your life?

2. In what area would you like to gain more control over your time?

3. What is your major time thief? What can you do to diminish its power over you?

4. Keep a log of your TV viewing for the next week. What does your log tell you about your use of time?

5. In what ways are *chronos* (the schedule and the tasks) and *kairos* (the special moments or experience) out of balance in your life? What can you do to bring these areas into balance?

One Person's
Reflections on Life

- *If my life were balanced, I would feel...* what is expressed in Ecclesiastes 3:1-8. There's a time for everything—a time to work and a time to relax; a time for schedule and a time for special moments. I would be at peace, knowing that God is God and that everything has its time. I would continually pray and give thanks to the Lord.

- *To me a fulfilled life means...* less stress. A peace that only the Lord Jesus can give. It's like turning a drinking glass upside down into a bathtub filled with water and no water getting in. it's like a shield. And Jesus is our shield of faith.

- *What keeps me from changing my life is...* that I sometimes get distracted, and I start to trust myself and my abilities instead of leaning on God. Even though I know this, I still do it.

- *If I were to have the life I really wanted, I would...* read the Word of God more. I would concentrate on what my heavenly Father has for me. I would concentrate on the love God has for me instead of worrying about what others think of me. Trying to get others' approval is exhausting. It's also not worth it.

3

The Hurry Illness

When we were children, we went to the doctor for a series of shots against smallpox, diphtheria, polio, and other illnesses. Do you remember? I sure do. And when you travel abroad to certain countries, you have to get shots to protect you from specific diseases.

Unfortunately, none of us received an inoculation for the disease that can hit all of us at one time or another. It's called "hurry sickness." It's a response that makes our internal clocks begin to run faster...and faster...and faster. As with any illness, specific symptoms reflect the presence of the illness. In the case of hurry sickness, the symptoms are heart disease, elevated blood pressure, and a depression of the immune system that makes you more susceptible to infections and cancer. These conditions are brought on when we exist in a state of stress, pressure, or constant rushing. Even tension headaches and ulcers are tied to hurry sickness. It's not the life experience we've always wanted.

Physically our bodies are deteriorating because we're living too fast. One of the growing physical problems today is Carpal Tunnel Syndrome (CTS). It's a condition of recurring, debilitating hand and wrist pain that develops from using these limbs for small, rapid, repetitive motions over an extended period of time. Assembly-line meat cutters, supermarket checkout clerks, and computer users are just some of those afflicted. The U.S. Department of Labor stated that in 1981, 18 percent of reported workplace injuries were CTS. But by 1988 the number had jumped to 48 percent. Who knows how bad it is today! The repetitive-motion disorder is a result of hurrying our bodies.

Rushing through life speeds up our natural body functions, and that damages our health. Most of us *are* sick. We have the hurry sickness. It's subtle and it doesn't sound any alarms. We catch it merely by living in our society.

How do you know if you've got it? Does this scenario sound familiar? You jump in the car for a trip. You've already called AAA to find out the fastest way to get to your destination. When you get to the freeway, you move over to the fast lane and set the cruise control for 65—the legal limit. But you don't stay there long. Everyone else is pushing 75 to 80. You try to see how quickly you can "get there."

We've been taught to rush through life. It starts in childhood with messages like "You've got to be on time," "Let's not dawdle," and "Try to come in first." At school you rushed to be the first out the door for recess or to go home. You didn't want to be known as the slow runner or a slow reader. You got rewarded for being first in line, the first one with the answer, the first one to put your hand up. "Be fast and make the best use of your time" is the message.

It's as if your life is on fast-forward. Graphologists have noted a difference in the scrawl of modern handwriting. Court reporters say witnesses now speak 20 to 40 words a minute faster than witnesses did 30 to 40 years ago.[1]

The trend toward a faster lifestyle isn't a recent change. In the 1920s, the key word was *quick*. Quick lunches, quick news summaries, quick-drying paint, quick Quaker oats. The hurry illness has been around for more than 80 years.

Faster Is Better?

The hectic life has intensified. Our standard for measurement has become the speed with which things are done. We speed-read. We have one-hour photo development and one-hour dry cleaning. If our fast food isn't ready in seven minutes, some restaurants promise that our food is free.[2]

We gauge the value of some of our appliances by how fast they are. We have speed dialing on our phones, super-speed blenders, and cars that go from 0 to 80 in 4.5 seconds. And if our computers take more than a minute to load a website, we impatiently drum our fingers and complain.

Does all of this speed enhance our lives? We may read faster, but does speed-reading brighten our enjoyment? Do modern conveniences save us time? They convert a few large, time-consuming tasks into many smaller ones that can actually take more time! Technology also raises our standards, so it takes more time to achieve what we expect.

On a flight between Los Angeles and Denver, I glanced through the airline magazine and noticed the ads related to time. One ad read, "I finished six books between New York and L.A.!" The ad went on to claim, "It's no exaggeration. With Soundview Executive Book Summaries you can slash hours off your reading time and gain a working knowledge of today's top business books quickly and easily. This is the executive solution to 'too much to read.' Absorb the key points of each book in 15 minutes. Save time!"

The message is "faster is better." But what are we rushing toward? And in our hurry, what might we leave behind?

Have you ever reached a point where you wanted to throw away the clock? Could you handle living for several days with no time pressure or with no means of telling time? For a number of years I have conducted a marriage seminar in Grand Teton National Park in Wyoming. At the beginning of our initial meeting on Sunday evening, I asked all participants to take off their watches and put them away for the evening—for three hours, that's all. And yet the expression on the faces of some of the participants and their hesitation spoke of the discomfort of going without a watch.

The Bulova watch company conducted an experiment in a small town in New Hampshire. All the residents left their watches off for two days and two nights. They had no way of keeping time. Some of them became disoriented. A few even said they didn't know if they were hungry or not because they didn't know whether or not it was mealtime. For me, that's hard to believe. I don't need a clock to know whether I'm hungry!

Some people have gone for months without a clock. At first, they keep checking their wrist to see the time, but after a while they develop their own rhythm.[3] But most of us are caught by the disrhythms and dysfunction of modern life—so much so that we rush through life without experiencing it.[4]

What Do We Lose?

The time-management books that tell us how to squeeze 48 hours out of a 24-hour day or how to pack every minute with as much productive activity as possible are not doing us any favors.

They're not really helping us simplify our lives and find balance. They're teaching us to produce more, do more, achieve more. Who says that *more* is what we want?

What do we lose when we hurry so much, when we concentrate on speed? In his book *More to Life Than Having It All,* Bob Welch says we lose a lot when we hurry through life:

> Hurrying means losing perspective. When we're so wrapped up in the stuff of life, we're too close to see the big picture. It's like looking closely at the screened photograph: All you see are fuzzy shades of gray. But when you take time to stand back, that tiny dot pattern becomes a picture with distinct blacks and whites. It becomes an image with meaning, a picture with a message. When was the last time you stepped back and surveyed the picture of your life?
>
> Hurrying means losing touch with those around you. Time is the soil in which relationships grow. Without time, our links to family, friends, and God all wither. Children take patience. Spouses take a listening ear. Friendships take follow-through. God takes our day-to-day attention.
>
> Hurrying means creating hurried children. Too many kids today are growing up without a childhood, forced to program their days as if they were pint-sized executives. We need to slow them down and allow them the innocence of youth, not push them into the adulthood that will come soon enough without our prodding.
>
> Hurrying means overlooking the value of processes. We have shifted from a process-oriented culture to a results-oriented culture. Strapped for time, we pay a fast-food restaurant to feed our family. We pay a childcare center to nurture our children. Some even pay a store clerk to do their gift shopping.[5]

Rushing and hurrying create a cluttered life rather than a simplified life.

Confusing Speed with Importance

Because our culture is obsessed with speed and hurrying, we have been duped into believing that every "urgent" matter is important. We live as if every event is a crisis. This adds to the hurry sickness. Perhaps you can identify with author Patrick Morley's insights about our frantic pace.

> Some days I feel bombarded with urgent requests for urgent answers to urgent problems that have urgent consequences. Some days I get the impression that the world will cease to spin on its axis unless I, Patrick Morley, personally take swift action. Sometimes, however, when I stop to analyze the significance of these seemingly weighty matters, I realize there is a lot of chaff, a little wheat and a great deal of chasing after the wind.
>
> Improvements in our telecommunications have resulted in our putting more pressure on each other, not less. The possibility of a speedy reply has only increased people's expectations. A few short years ago you could take a couple of weeks to think about a major decision. Today people expect you to think, ruminate, consider, decide and fax them your "wise" answer in five minutes! When we move so fast, we lose the value of letting a decision "sit" for a season. Wisdom gets watered down. Creativity gets cut short. Blood pressure gets a spike.
>
> Each of us operates best at a particular pace. When we let our communication devices determine our pace, we invariably run too fast. After all, going faster captures the whole purpose of these devices! We need to set our thermostat and

control our own pace, rather than react like a thermom-
eter that merely adjusts to the demands of whoever clamors
the loudest and most persistently. We have the *technological*
capacity to make ourselves available at a level that we may
not have the *physical* capacity to service. Yes, instant access
is a good thing, but only when used with wisdom.[6]

Does Morley's description fit your life at all? Do you feel the
pressure that technology places on you? Do you feel as if you're
always panting to keep up? Again, we have to ask ourselves what
we gain and what we lose with this pace. We may gain some sense
of instant contact with people when we can fax them or reach them
on their cell phones, to talk about decisions that need to be made.
But what do we lose? As Morley says, we lose that thinking time,
the reflection time, the time to come to wise decisions.

Stress

With the fast pace of life, we end up feeling wound up like we're
being twisted tighter and tighter. In other words, we're stressed. Yes,
stress is a common, catchall word to describe the tension and pressure we often feel. But do you really understand what stress is?

Stress is the irritation you feel in any bothersome life situation. The Latin word for stress is *strictus.* It means "to be drawn
tight." In Old French the word is *estresse,* which means "narrow-
ness" or "tightness." Stress is anything that places conflicting or
heavy demands on you. Hurrying creates stress, and when you feel
pressure, your body quickly mobilizes its defenses for fight or flight.
In the case of stress, we're flooded with an abundance of adrenaline, which disrupts normal functioning and creates a heightened
sense of arousal.

A stressed person is like a rubber band that is being stretched.

When the pressure is released, the rubber band returns to normal. But if it's stretched too much or too long, the rubber begins to lose its elastic qualities, becomes brittle, develops some cracks, and eventually breaks. That's what happens to us if we have too much stress, too much hurrying in our lives.

What's stressful to one person may not be stressful to another. Some people get stressed about unavoidable future events. Other people feel stress after certain events have occurred. For still other people, stress is the wear and tear of life. They feel like pieces of stone that have been hammered at for so long that they begin to crumble.

Slowing Down

We need to place speed limits on our lives. The speed limits on our highways have a purpose—to save our lives. If we drive too fast, we can make mistakes, lose control, and have a life-changing accident. The speed limit helps us maintain a pace that's safe, sane, and steady.

We need to find the safe speed for our lives. We've come to believe that we have to hurry because we don't have enough time. But could hurrying be the reason we don't have enough time? People who are in a hurry never have enough time and never seem to gain enough so that they don't have to hurry. Think about it. Hurry brings on stress, lack of enjoyment in what you're doing, and the tendency to make mistakes.

In his book *Zorba the Greek,* Nikos Kazantzakis relates a poignant story that taught him a painful lesson about rushing.

> I remember one morning when I discovered a cocoon in the bark of a tree, just as the butterfly was making a hole in its case and preparing to come out. I waited a while, but

it was too long appearing, and I was impatient. I bent over it and breathed on it to warm it. I warmed it as quickly as I could, and the miracle began to happen before my eyes faster than life. The cocoon opened. The butterfly started crawling out, and I shall never forget my horror when I saw how its wings were folded back and crumpled; the wretched butterfly tried with its whole trembling body to unfold them. Bending over it I tried to help it with my breath, in vain. It needed to be hatched patiently. And the unfolding of the wings should be a gradual process in the sun. Now it was too late. My breath had forced the butterfly to appear all crumpled before its time. It struggled desperately and a few seconds later died in the palm of my hand.

That little body is, I do believe, the greatest weight I have on my conscience. For I realized today that it is a mortal sin to violate the great laws of nature. We should not hurry. We should not be impatient. But we should confidently obey the eternal rhythm. If only that little butterfly could always flutter before me to show me the way.[7]

Hurrying isn't the answer. It won't help. It won't work. It will stress you out more and build a sense of panic. What you want to do is slow down. Yes, that's what I said: *Slow down!* In fact, when your day is coming apart and you're running around in circles, stop. Hold everything. Sit down in a comfortable chair. Take a deep breath and...read the following prayer:

Steady my hurried pace with a vision of the eternal reach of time.

Give me, amid the confusion of the day, the calmness of everlasting hills.

Break the tensions of my nerves and muscles with the soothing music of the singing streams that live in my memory.

Teach me the art of taking minute vacations—of slowing down to look at a flower, to chat with a friend, to pat a dog, to smile at a child, to read a few lines from a good book.

Slow me down, Lord, and inspire me to send my roots deep into the soil of life's enduring values, that I may grow toward my greater destiny.

Remind me each day that the race is not always to the swift, that there is more to life than increasing speed.

Let me look upward to the towering oak and know that it grew great and strong because it grew slowly and well.[8]

What can you do about rushing through life and avoiding the time crunch? What can you do to slow down?

We've been taught to accelerate in order to accomplish more. Maybe it's time to realize that pushing harder and faster wears out our bodies. Deceleration will help us handle our time in a better way. How? Try these things for starters.

- Do nothing from time to time, and discover it's all right to do so.

- Ask, "Do I really have to rush? What is the worst that can happen if I don't? And if I do?"

- Call time-outs throughout the day.

- Welcome delays as an opportunity to relax.

- If you're rushing, cut your speed in half.

- Stop frequently, take a deep breath, and say, "I don't have to be in such a hurry."

- Listen to your body.

- Finally (and this may raise your anxiety level at first), reduce your awareness of time. Carry a card with you for a day and indicate with a check mark two things: how often you check the time and how often you are hurrying.

- Put most of your clocks out of sight and take off your watch for a day. Don't ask other people about the time, and don't listen to the radio station that gives the time frequently.

  You will soon discover that the less often you check the time, the better your own sense of time will become.[9]

You know, it's not very relaxing or enjoyable to be around frantic, fast-paced people, even if they are Christians. We weren't called to live like this. Tim Hansel puts it well:

> We are called to be faithful, not frantic….I believe that the Enemy has done an effective job of convincing us that unless a person is worn to a frazzle, running here and there, he or she cannot possibly be a dedicated, sacrificing, spiritual Christian. Perhaps the Seven Deadly Sins have recruited another member—Overwork.
>
> We need to remember that our strength lies not in hurried efforts and ceaseless long hours, but in our quietness and confidence.
>
> The world today says, "Enough is not enough."
> Christ softly answers, "Enough is enough."[10]

As you work toward a fulfilled life, consider these final thoughts. When you read this chapter, did you rush through it or take it leisurely? Are you speed-reading this book? If you looked at your life as if you were running a race, what kind would it be—a marathon or a sprint? If you are sprinting too often, ask the Lord to show you how to slow down and get more out of your life.

Time for Reflection

What is your life like at this time? Is it disrupted and chaotic or is it harmonious and in balance? You may find your answer as you respond to these questions.

1. At the end of the day, do you feel frustrated and exhausted because you don't have very much to show for your efforts?

2. Do you end up rushing to get things done on time at work and at home because of interruptions, crises, and unreasonable deadlines?

3. Do you feel immobilized because of too many commitments?

4. Do you run through your day at a fast rate, wishing you could go faster?

5. Do you end up feeling guilty or angry because of what you haven't accomplished?

6. What about those important projects? Do you tend to put them off because you're too rushed?

7. Is there any sense of compulsion to what you do? What might your answers say about the rate at which you're going through life?

One Person's
Reflections on Life

- *If my life were balanced, I would*…feel less pressed, less hurried, less confused. I would be a healthier person, free to do what God wants me to do. I would also feel closer to God.

- *To me a fulfilled life means*…living a life that has a rhythm—waking up with sunrise, eating simple healthy food, putting in a good day's work, believing the best about others, falling asleep with thanksgiving in my heart.

- *What keeps me from changing my life is*…the pace that technology sets for our lives. I feel breathless. My family and friends live in various towns, so I need to travel to see them. But the problem is really me. I have allowed the enemy to persuade me that the things of this world are harmless and that I somehow need them in order to be even more blessed. The truth is that these things actually put a wall between me and God.

- *If I were to have the life I really wanted, I would*…get rid of all the materialistic things that distract me from God's Word and all other unnecessary possessions that prevent me from truly living by the power of the Spirit. I would also get rid of the answering machine and television. I would work nine to five on weekdays and rest on weekends. I would live in a town where I didn't need a car and where I could walk to the store, bank, work, family, and friends. Doesn't that sound heavenly?

4

How Do We Measure Success?

Success. It drives us, stymies us, frustrates us, eludes us, dominates us. Let's admit it. We all want to be successful at something. We are taught to be successful. We're told we need to be successful. We live in a success-dominated society. We're urged to "go for it."

One of the best-known football coaches of all time, Vince Lombardi, said, "Winning isn't everything—it's the *only* thing!" He applied that to football. Others apply it to life. We're always trying to succeed at something. But like anything else, our striving for success can be out of balance. Success can become addictive. It can even destroy us. Is success the dream you've been chasing? Is this the life you've always wanted?

Listen to these perspectives on success:

Aristotle Onassis, tycoon: "It's not a question of money. After you reach a certain point, money becomes most unimportant. What matters is success. The sensible thing would be for me to stop now. But I can't. I have to keep aiming higher and higher—just for the thrill."

Barbara Streisand, recording artist: "Success for me is having ten honeydew melons and eating only the top half of each one."

Ted Turner, media mogul: "Well, I think it's kind of an empty bag, to tell you the truth, but you have to really get there to really know that. I've always said I was more an adventurer than I was a businessman. I mainly did CNN just to see if it would work. And the same with the superstation…just out of personal curiosity to see if it could be done."[1]

How do you measure success?

- Having a good job?
- Owning your own home?
- Earning a professional degree?
- Having a meaningful marriage?
- Traveling to exciting places?
- Getting a promotion?
- Driving the car of your dreams?
- Having a vacation home?
- Reaching the top of your career ladder?
- Salting away a sizable retirement account?
- Being involved in meaningful ministry?

- To know Christ and to make Him known (Philippians 3:10)?

Do you feel pressured to succeed? Who has placed that pressure on you? How is your life complicated?

One of the ways we can get balance in our lives and have the lives we want is to change our expectations of ourselves, of others, of life. We do this by evaluating our expectations and by evaluating *whose* expectations we are trying to meet.

Do you measure success for yourself—or do you allow others to determine it for you? If it's the latter, you may feel as if you're living out someone else's life. It's one more way of allowing your life to be controlled by other people. So perhaps you're the one who needs to set what it means for you to be successful. But even that isn't true. God is the one who has the plan for you. (More about this later.)

Does Success Satisfy?

When you consider yourself successful, do you *feel* successful? Many struggle with the "Empty Success Syndrome." They have all the apparent success symbols but none of the satisfaction. Feeling empty in the midst of abundance isn't the way it's supposed to be.

Success is a subjective, inner perception. You may have heard the story about three baseball umpires who were asked how they call balls and strikes. One said, "I simply call them the way I see them." Another said, "I just call them the way they are." But the last one said, "They're nothing until I call them." The issue here is perception. If your inner response fails to match up with your outward signs of success, pay attention to the message.

There's also a price tag attached to success. Some participants at an auction are willing to bid any amount to get what they want. Some people approach success the same way. Success without counting the cost or success that costs too much may not really be success. *The Executive Digest* said, "The trouble with success is the formula is the same as the one for a nervous breakdown." That's sobering. That's uncomfortable. And it's too often true.

The way you achieve success may violate your own values so much that what you attain feels tainted. This causes you to see yourself in a negative way. An Old Testament story describes this process. David wanted Bathsheba, but she was another man's wife. After David got her pregnant, he had her husband killed so he could marry her. David was "successful." But when the Lord sent the prophet Nathan to confront him, David experienced tremendous guilt. Many of us end up the same way.

What happens to you after you reach your goal of being successful? Is it elation or depression? Is it sufficient and satisfying... or do you need more? Have you ever reached your goal, looked around, and said, "Is this all there is?" That's the condition known as Executive Promotion Depression. Success can be lonely. It can also be empty. Once it's over, then what? Some personalities are so goal oriented that reaching the goal is all that's important. They don't savor the process. We can be satisfied either from the process of reaching the goal or just the goal itself. Success is a *process* as well as a result.

How Do You Define Success?

Ron Jenson, author of *Make a Life, Not Just a Living,* raises several possibilities of how people define success: power, prosperity, position, prestige, pleasure.

Power

Power motivates many. We see it in families, businesses, and even churches. Some judge themselves to be successful if they have the power to make decisions or the power to earn lots of money or the power to control others.

How important is power to you? Before you dismiss the question, think about it. Do you seek power in your relationships? In your workplace?

Prosperity

Is success prosperity? Some people become preoccupied with the accumulation of things. The title of a book published a few years ago—*Kids Who Have Too Much* by Ralph Minear—is a commentary on our contemporary consumer mentality. As I work with people in premarital counseling, I repeatedly see couples who expect to start out financially at a point it took their parents 30 years to reach. Couples today feel a sense of entitlement, especially when it comes to money.

Too often we equate success with accumulation. We think that the more we have, the more successful we are. In his book *If I'm Not Tarzan and My Wife Isn't Jane, Then What Are We Doing in the Jungle?* Steve Farrar shares an interesting description of the accumulation that complicates our lives. In the early 1900s many people died in influenza epidemics. While families are rarely destroyed by influenza epidemics today, they are at high risk of another epidemic: *affluenza*.[2]

The lyrics to this song describe affluenza:

> Now I lay me down to sleep;
> I pray my Cuisinart to keep.
> I pray my stocks are on the rise,
> And that my analyst is wise,
> That all the wine I sip is white

> And that my hot tub's watertight,
> That racquetball won't get too tough,
> That all my sushi's fresh enough.
> I pray my cordless phone still works,
> That my career won't lose its perks,
> My microwave won't radiate,
> My condo won't depreciate.
> I pray my health club doesn't close
> And that my money market grows.
> If I go broke before I wake,
> I pray my Volvo they won't take![3]

What are the symptoms of affluenza?

- Desiring to have more, regardless of what we have.

- Striving to be successful without being contented.

- Placing career over family.

- Refusing to be satisfied with less than the best.

- Refusing to follow the biblical guidelines to live our lives to God's glory.[4]

Do any of these symptoms reflect your experience? Has affluenza infected your family? It's contagious, you know. Our contact with cultural values alone puts us in danger of catching affluenza. We need to be on guard, to inoculate ourselves against the illness. Part of the inoculation comes from taking an honest look at where we are. We can simplify our lives only when we face our drive for success, our press for significance, our need for more.

Having more is not always a good thing says Gary Aumiller, author of *Keeping It Simple:*

The devices and the toys that we have adorned ourselves with in the past two decades to entertain, amuse, make life *more* convenient, or attempt to make ourselves happier are truly amazing. Children…will experience or have already experienced "things" that could not even have been imagined by children of previous decades. Yet, although these generations will have all this and *more,* I believe that they will be the poorest of generations when it comes to appreciating real pleasures. *More* will add up to more stress, more broken relationships, more distance from one's own spirit.

How can more mean less? When the possession of *more* costs a disproportionate amount in life's complications than it produces in life's pleasures. When you spend a disproportionate amount of time earning and maintaining the "things" or *more* than is spent enjoying those "things." When you spend *more* time examining the complexities of your life than enjoying the activities of your life. When spirituality adds *more* hassles to your life and seems to miss the real meaning. When *more* separates you from the people you love rather than bringing you together. When you spend more time thinking how to feel good than you do feeling good.[5]

Most people today want what they *don't* have more than what they *do* have. A man I know described his adventure with wristwatches. He's enamored with them. When watches with built-in alarms first came out, he had to have one. When waterproof watches became available, he became dissatisfied with his alarm wristwatch and bought a waterproof watch. Finally he was satisfied. Until a few months later, when a catalog advertised a new watch—a waterproof alarm watch. He immediately bought one. When he learned about digital watches that could beep every hour—you guessed it—he bought one. Ah, but soon after that the technology exploded, and he needed a watch with a calculator and one that could measure temperature and one that could store phone numbers and even one that could measure his heartbeat. It never ends.

You may not be seduced into buying watches, but what is it for you? Some people need to buy an abundance of clothes. Others need the latest model car. Still others may have the computer with the latest chip and the latest software. We focus on what we don't have and say, "I must have that. I need it." But the truth is that we don't need it—we *want* it. The truth also is that accumulating these things doesn't satisfy. God's Word has something to say to us about our need to accumulate things.

> Don't weary yourself trying to get rich. Why waste your time? (Proverbs 23:4).

> Those who love money will never have enough. How absurd to think that wealth brings true happiness! (Ecclesiastes 5:10).

> But people who long to be rich fall into temptation and are trapped by many foolish and harmful desires that plunge them into ruin and destruction (1 Timothy 6:9).

> No one can serve two masters. For you will hate one and love the other, or be devoted to one and despise the other. You cannot serve both God and money (Luke 16:13).

These verses are helpful directives and, at the same time, strong warnings. Financial success will not satisfy us. Instead of focusing on what we don't have, we need to look at what we do have, identify what it is doing for us, and thank God for it.[6]

Position and Prestige

Two other definitions of success, according to Ron Jenson, are position and prestige. Could your definition of success be one of these? Are degrees and titles important to you? Are you trying to "make a name for yourself"? When you are part of a group, do you feel slighted if you are not chosen to be a leader, to be the visible one? Many people live for status and its symbols: a house in the "right" neighborhood, the "right" car, the "right" friends. But in the end, these things don't satisfy. And interestingly enough, the greater the visibility, the higher the risk of being hurt, criticized, slandered, and misunderstood.

And Ron's last category?

Pleasure

Do you define success by how much pleasure you experience? Pleasure seeking is an active pursuit for many people. We look for pleasure in food, in entertainment, in travel, and in many other ways. Pleasure seeking is nothing new. It's not lasting either. It's a bit like drinking or taking drugs. As you go along, you need to take more and more to be satisfied.[7]

Perhaps you're uncomfortable as you look at these descriptions of success. They hit home. I've seen people who have all of these things, and eventually they get to the place where they ask, "There's more than this, isn't there? There's got to be."

Here's some good news. You can change the direction of your pursuit and unclutter your life. Most people know the name Alfred Nobel, the man for whom the Nobel Peace Prize was named. But not too many people know his story. He invented dynamite and made a fortune from it, as well as from other powerful explosives used for weapons. A number of years later, Nobel's brother died.

But whoever wrote the obituary confused Alfred and his brother and wrote an obituary for Alfred. The obituary described Alfred as a man who made his fortune by enabling people to kill others in large numbers. Alfred Nobel was shocked and shaken when he read that. It caused him to reassess his life and what he had been doing. He decided to use his fortune to honor accomplishments that were beneficial to society and humanity. So he created the Nobel Peace Prize.

Will You Know Success When You See It?

Our view of success reflects our values. All of us—parents, students, ministers, gang members, police officers, burglars—are driven by what we value. Our values are reflected in what we give our lives to. They're reflected in the way we use our time and energy.

A fisherman lying on the bank of a river in Maine was having a great time. He'd cast his line into the gently moving water, and now and then he'd catch a silver salmon. He had his lunch and beverage by his side as he sat in the shade of a tree. His stringer was getting heavy with the weight of the fish.

He was bringing in another large fish when a well-dressed businessman drove up, got out of the car, and came over to him. "Don't you know that you could catch many more fish if you put several lines into the water?" he asked.

The fisherman replied, "Why would I want more fish?"

"Well, look, it's simple," the businessman said. "If you had more lines, you'd catch more fish and make more money. And then if you made more money, you could buy a fishing boat. Once you did that, you could open up a store and sell your fish to everyone. After you open one store, you could open several others. You'd employ many people, and eventually you could become a fish wholesaler and ship fish all over the country. And then you would become very wealthy."

The fisherman took a bite of his sandwich and looked skeptically at the businessman. "And then what would I do?" he asked.

"Well, if you became that successful, you'd have all the time you wanted to do what you enjoy the most. You could lie back, relax, and go fishing."

The fisherman smiled and said, "But that's what I'm doing now."

This fisherman's values were reflected in how he used his time. He knew he was successful even though it wasn't apparent to others. He knew that his success was not measured by how much he owned or how much money he had but by his sense of inner contentment. The fisherman knew that success is something internal rather than external.[8]

Are you like the fisherman? Will you know success when you see it or will you keep pursuing an illusion? Terry Hershey says, "We live in a weird world where more is never enough. We cannot be content, so we fantasize about those who do 'arrive' by reading about lifestyles of rich and famous people; we sacrifice the values of our 'ordinary life' of relationships, family and personal solitude to pursue the ecstasy of that which will let us 'be somebody.'"[9] The fisherman knew he was somebody. He had found his ecstasy in simple pleasure.

The problem with the pursuit of ecstasy is that you also feel as if you're on a bungee cord much of the time. Perhaps an example of this is a top-rated disc jockey who operates in both Dallas and Chicago. That's right, Dallas and Chicago—each day! He's in Dallas in the morning and Chicago in the afternoon. He commutes 2,000 miles every day and works the weekend events, too. Oh, he's compensated for it all right, in the range of $600,000 to $700,000 per year.

Each day he begins just before five-thirty on the Dallas radio station K104 to do his three-and-a-half hour morning drive-time show. As soon as he's done with that show, at nine o-clock, he's on his way to Dallas–Fort Worth International Airport. He runs into the airport, flashes his $150,000 American Airlines Airpass, and takes a seat in first class. He has his lunch and briefcase with him. He arrives at Chicago's O'Hare Airport, gets into his waiting limousine, and goes to a local health club for a quick workout, and then on to the WGCI studio for the afternoon commute crowd from two o'clock until six. (Aren't you worn out just reading about his schedule?) Then he has a frantic drive back to O'Hare for a flight that arrives in Dallas at nine o'clock. He's in bed by eleven, only to start all over again when the alarm goes off at three thirty the next morning.[10]

Is this success? Many people would say yes. But this disc jockey certainly pays a physical, emotional, and relational toll for his schedule, his choices, and his "success."

One thing we would all agree about: There's nothing *simple* about his lifestyle.

Finding Success Through Failure

How about Gary Paulsen? Was he a success? You decide after you hear his story.

Paulsen lived in Minnesota, where he played around with dog-sledding a bit. After putting in just 150 training miles with his dogsled, he ran the grueling Alaskan Iditarod dogsled race—1200 miles from Anchorage to Nome.

The first day Paulsen began training was a preview of what he might expect as a novice in the race. He went from one disaster to another. He hitched up his dogs, waved to his wife, and jerked loose the rope holding the sled to a tree. The dogs took off like a shot. It felt as if the sled hit the ground only every few feet. When the dogs came to the end of the driveway and needed to make a turn onto the road, they turned the corner well, but Paulsen forgot to lean as the sled rounded the corner. The sled overturned, but the dogs kept running. By this time Paulsen was under the sled dragging on the gravel! Four miles later he was able to get the sled up on its wheels. A handlebar was gone, and most of his clothes were shredded from the dragging. He said he was never once in control of that 30-mile training run that day.

Other days weren't much better. He left the yard on his face, his rear, his back, and his belly. One day he forgot about some wooden matches in his back pocket. You guessed it! He fell on his rear and was pulled along, igniting the matches and giving him the look of a flaming meteorite shooting down the driveway.

But despite all of his training fiascoes, Paulsen made it to the race. And he finished. He said he would come back the next year and win.

He did return. He didn't win.[11]

I'll ask the question again: Was Paulsen a success? Or was he a failure because he didn't win?

Have you ever heard James Earl Jones' voice? You may remember him from the movie *Field of Dreams* or as the voice of Mufasa, the father lion, in *The Lion King*, or as the voice of Darth Vader in the three *Star Wars* films. Jones has won three Emmy Awards, two Tony Awards, a Golden Globe, and a Grammy. But it wasn't always like that.

When James Earl Jones was 14 years old, he stuttered so badly that he never spoke in class. He was awkward, shy, and socially isolated. He communicated with others through notes. One day his teacher asked him to read a poem aloud in front of class. When Jones overcame his fear and began to read, the words began to flow. He liked it and wanted to do more. So he practiced again and again. Through his speaking ability, he won competitions and eventually a college scholarship. For years he worked playing small roles in off-Broadway productions and supported himself as a janitor. But he never, never gave up. He admits that what he learned through his early disappointments and failures played a major role in who he is today.[12]

We don't like to fail. We don't even like to use the word. But failure and success go hand in hand. In so many cases, failure comes before great discoveries. Remember this: A failure or mistake carries with it the opportunity to make a change that will get us on the right track. We all fail. We all make mistakes. But have you considered how God can take those mistakes and bring some good out of them?

Alexander Fleming was a research physician who appeared to make a mistake one day. He left a window open, and some mold blew in and contaminated a bacteria culture in a dish. He could have thrown up his hands in frustration and thrown out the contaminated dish. Instead, Fleming decided to observe what would happen to the bacteria. Something in the mold produced a substance that prevented staphylococcus growth. He named the substance penicillin. It has healed millions. A mistake? Yes. A failure? No.[13]

Gary Oliver, author of *How to Get It Right After You've Gotten It Wrong*, makes an important observation about failure: "Failures can leave many different scars—hurt feelings, wounded relationships, wasted potential, broken marriages, shattered ministries—but they can also be used by God to sharpen the mind, deepen the spirit and strengthen the soul. Those people who have learned to view failure through God's eyes emerge with a softer heart, stronger character, and a fresh awareness of God's grace."[14]

What feels like failure can, in God's skilled hands, become a part of his provision for our growth. We can't be successful in the Christian life if we deny the existence of failure. If we learn how to value it, understand it, and take it to the foot of the Cross, we can become wiser and stronger because of it.[15]

The Biblical Measure of Success

The definition of success comes back to expectations. What do we expect from ourselves? What do other people expect from us? Whose standard is important? When our expectations of ourselves are shaped by the measurement devices of our popular culture, we will often "fail." But when our expectations are shaped by biblical values, we find ourselves straining less and feeling less pressure to come out on top.

What is the biblical measure of success? When God was preparing Joshua to lead the Israelites into the Promised Land, he laid out for Joshua the criteria: "Obey all the laws Moses gave you. Do not turn away from them, and you will be successful in everything you do. Study this Book of the Law continually. Meditate on it day and night so you may be sure to obey all that is written in it. Only then will you succeed" (Joshua 1:7-8). There it is—obedience.

We are successful when we obey God's Word, when we are faithful to what he calls us to do. Will that always involve success as the rest of the world defines it? Often not. But it will lead to contentment and a sense of satisfaction that we have done the right thing. That may do more for having the life you've always wanted then you could ever imagine.

In his book *Guard Your Heart,* Gary Rosberg describes success in an appealing way:

Success is not just a matter of money, power, and ego, but also issues of the heart—like compassion, kindness, bravery, generosity, love.

It's an issue of character, not performance.

It's an issue of being the person God designed you to be, not how much salary you can pull down in a year.

It's an issue of who you really are, not how many notches you can rack up on your resumé or the shape of your car's hood ornament.

There's a shift now in our culture. Success hasn't cut it. But significance has more meaning.

Who makes us significant? I believe it is a Person. Not your boss, kids, parents, or even you. What makes you and me significant is the Person of Jesus Christ. He created us in order to glorify Himself. That's our job in life, to bring honor and glory to Him. He is the One who makes us significant.[16]

Consider God's Word: "Since we find ourselves fashioned into all these excellently formed and marvelously functioning parts in Christ's body, let's just go ahead and be what we were made to be" (Romans 12:5 MSG).

There's an old Danish proverb that says, "What you are is God's gift to you; what you do with yourself is your gift to God."

God deserves your best. He shaped you for a purpose, and he expects you to make the most of what you have been given. He doesn't want you to worry about or covet abilities you don't have. Instead he wants you to focus on talents he has given you to use.

When you attempt to serve God in ways you're not shaped to serve, it feels like forcing a square peg into a round hole. It's frustrating and produces limited results. It also wastes your time, your talent, and your energy. The best use of your life is to serve God out of your shape. To do this you must discover your shape, learn to accept and enjoy it, and then develop it to its fullest potentital.[17]

If our personal expectations are shaped by God's expectations, we'll feel free. We won't be pressed by unrealistic cultural standards. We will find ourselves contented, centered, and able to discover the life we've always wanted. If God chose to write a letter about success and his expectations of you, what might he say? In *The Seven Seasons of a Man's Life*, Patrick Morley suggests that such a letter might look like this:

Dear Son,

I am writing because I want you to stop and take stock of your life. I want you to look closely at the ways you have lived your life. I want you to make changes based on a new commitment to My larger purposes for your life and the world—while you still have time.

I am going to give you some things to ponder. Do this in a quiet place either early in the morning or late at night, when it is still and quiet. Don't be in a rush. Give yourself plenty of time. Think it over.

You have wanted success. Success is elusive, isn't it? That's because you have been living by your own ideas. I do want you to be successful, but on My terms, not yours. You measure success in the quantity of your possessions and achievements. I measure success in the quality of your character and conduct. You are interested in the success of your soul. True success is to satisfy your calling, not your ambition. Live as a called man.

He is successful who is found faithful to do the will of God. Are you seeking to know and do My will? Or are you succeeding in a way that doesn't really matter to Me? Would you be willing to live the rest of your life in obscurity if that is My will?

I made you with dignity. I created you to be significant. I have put in you the spark of divinity. You are My crowning achievement. You are the full expression of My creative genius. You are My most excellent creation. I was at My very best when I created you. Do you understand and believe what I have just said?

Be careful not to overemphasize either your significance or your insignificance. If you think too highly of yourself, you will lose your humility and brokenness before Me and think there is nothing you cannot do. Are you a humble or proud man? Answer carefully. Or if you think too little of yourself, you will not love yourself and your neighbors. You will be afraid to try something bold. At the end of their lives most men wish they had been more bold. Do you love yourself? Do you love your neighbors? Do you need to be more bold for Me?

The biggest problem I see in your life is that you have spent your whole life looking for something worth living for. It would be better if you found something worth dying for. Give your life to that, and I will give you joy, no matter how hard the path becomes. What is the cause you would be willing to die for? Better still, who is the one you would be willing to die for? How, then, should you reorder your life?

I want you to reflect carefully on what I am about to say. Success that really matters depends on a few key areas: having a close, moment-by-moment walk with Me, finding fulfilling work, modeling a life of integrity, living within your means, maintaining your health (My temple), establishing loving relationships, living a life of good deeds, and coming to live with Me when you die.

What changes should you make in the brief time you have remaining? How would you live if I told you that you have only one year left on earth? One month? One week? One day?

Live your life in the shadow of the cross. Soon, My son, you will see Me face-to-face.

> Eternally yours,
> Your heavenly Father[18]

It's something to think about.

Time for Reflection

1. What has been your definition of success over the years, and how did you develop this?

2. What is your greatest struggle with success? How has it complicated your life?

3. How has failure affected your life and helped you experience success?

4. What are your personal expectations of success?

5. What do you feel are other people's expectations of you?

6. What do you think are God's expectations of you?

7. How would having a biblical view of success help you simplify your life?

One Person's
Reflections on Life

- *If my life were centered on Him, I would feel…*like living each day as more of a blessing. With God's guidance, I would value the right things. My life would be less cluttered, and I would be able to concentrate on the areas I really care about.

- *To me a fulfilled life means…*having a positive perspective—yes, that's what a simplified lifestyle is all about. This happens when I know the real meaning of success and have identified the important areas of my life.

- *If I were to change my focus, I would…*let go of my ideas of success and learn more about God's plan for my life. I would try to live in the present and find more time for solitude, reflection, learning, and awareness.

5

Living with Balanced Priorities

Balance is all around us. Watch the tightrope walker make his way across the taut cable stretched from one building to another. His very life is dependent on staying in balance. In the movie *The Karate Kid*, the elderly instructor Miyagi sends Daniel, his young student, into the breaking surf with the admonition, "Learn balance! Learn balance!" Again and again the boy is knocked off his feet by the breaking waves. All at once he sees what balance is as he views Mr. Miyagi standing on top of a single slender post. While up there, Miyagi performs the crane technique, which is very intricate. Easily he shifts in midair from one foot to the other. His body is in perfect balance.

We all want balance in our lives. None of us disagrees about that. We know that achieving and maintaining balance helps us get more out of life. But the problems come in deciding what is out of balance, what we can do to correct the imbalance, and what we can do to maintain the balance. Before we explore the dynamics of achieving and maintaining balance, take some time to evaluate your situation:

- What two areas do you already know are out of balance in your life?
- What two areas do you feel are in healthy balance?
- What's the most difficult thing for you to balance? Time? responsibilities? relationships? expectations? priorities?
- How does the lack of balance complicate your life?
- How would finding balance help you simplify your life?
- Can you have the life you've always wanted if your life is out of balance?

Your answers to these questions will guide your exploration of the material in this chapter.

Finding balance is a personal challenge for most people today. The challenges we face in this country aren't from scarcity but from surplus. We don't struggle as much with absence in our lives as with abundance. Most of us find that our struggle isn't for basic survival—food and shelter—but to get every family member together. One of the best statements I've found to depict the problem with our cluttered lives comes from the book *Lifebalance:* "It's not the sparse simplicity of too little but the crowded complexity of too much that plagues our lives. And the answers lie not in the balance of our abilities but in our ability to balance!"[1]

Let's look at four important areas that may help you in your search for balance. These areas are: threats to balance, balanced priorities, balanced attitudes, and balanced expectations.

Threats to Balance

What makes balance so hard to achieve and maintain? What

are the obstacles we must recognize and overcome? Our sense of balance is often threatened by pressures that seem urgent. Urgency itself is not the problem. We all face urgent times. But when urgency becomes the motivating factor, then it's an addiction.

I see mothers who operate their lives from an urgency addiction. I see men in all professions operate their lives from urgency addictions. They live their lives in crisis-management mode. Some people like it. They feel useful, fulfilled, successful and needed. But when the crisis calms down, what then? Some people are so addicted to the by-product of the crises that they have to create a new crisis. Their lives are out of sync, out of balance.

What is urgent may not be what is most important. And this is why our lives become complicated. In the classic book *Tyranny of the Urgent,* author Charles Hummel says:

> The important rarely must be done today, or even this week.... The urgent tasks call for instant action.... The momentary appeal of these tasks seems irresistible and important, and they devour our energy. But in the light of time's perspective, their deceptive prominence fades; with a sense of loss we recall the vital task we pushed aside. We realize we've become slaves to the tyranny of the urgent.[2]

Think about your own life and answer these questions:

- When you're feeling out of balance, are you ruled by the tyranny of the urgent?
- Why do you do what you do?
- What motivates you?
- What prompts or drives you?

A second threat to our balance is overload. Often our lives feel out of balance because they are cluttered, full of too much. We have too many options, too many opportunities, too many good things. But too much of a good thing is not positive. We can blame the overload on our society, the schools, work, church, and our families. But that's not it. The problem is us— our reaction, our response, our willingness to let ourselves become influenced or controlled by everything around us. The apostle Paul's words echo in our mind: "Do not be conformed to this world" or "Don't let the world around you squeeze you into its own mould" (Romans 12:2 NASB and PHILLIPS).

Balanced Priorities

An instructor at a seminar told the participants to pre-pare for a quiz. He reached under the table and took out a wide-mouth gallon jar and set it on the table. Next to the jar were a number of fist-sized rocks. He asked the group, "How many of these rocks do you think we can get inside this jar?" The participants began to make their guesses. The instructor said, "Let's find out." One by one he began to put as many rocks as he could into the jar until the rocks inside were level with the top of the jar.

The instructor asked, "Is the jar full?" All the participants looked at the jar filled with rocks and said it was.

But then the instructor took out a bucket of gravel, poured it into the jar, and shook it. The gravel drifted down into all the little crevices and spaces around the rocks. The instructor asked once again, "Is the jar full?"

The participants were not about to be fooled a second time. They said that the jar probably wasn't full.

The instructor nodded and said, "Good. You are catching on." He next took out a bucket of sand and proceeded to pour it into the jar. Slowly the sand began to fill in all the gaps and holes left by the gravel. After the sand settled, the instructor once again asked, "Now, is the jar full?"

The participants were much more emphatic this time when they said, "No!"

The instructor was pleased they were beginning to understand an important principle. He took a pitcher of water and poured a quart into the jar. At this point he stopped and asked the group, "What's the point of this?"

One of the participants said, "There are gaps, and if you work at it you can always fit more into the jar."

But the instructor said, "No, that's not really the point. It's this: If I had not put in those big rocks first, I would never have gotten them in."[3]

Perhaps this is what many of us do. We don't consider what to do first, so we end up devoting too much time to things that are not important. The result is we have little time left for the most significant issues in life. The priorities we select are not really priorities. Many of us take the approach the one participant suggested. We keep juggling so we can fit more into our lives. That's why we're out of balance. Perhaps what we see as the most urgent gets the most attention even if it isn't the most vital. For many who are faced with multitudes of options, choices, opportunities, and alternatives, the tension lies in deciding what really *is* the most important.

We also feel tension between internal and external priorities. Gordon MacDonald, author of *Ordering Your Private World,* says our private world—the part we don't reveal to very many people—is usually a neglected world. We spend more time trying to manage our outer world and fail to realize the significant connection between the two. Most of us spend our time shaping and tending what's visible to others. It's easier to deal with this part of life because it's measurable. But our inner world involves our values. Sometimes that is where the real battles of life occur.

Perhaps when we want to know how our friends are doing, we should learn to ask two separate questions. The first (the one we usually ask) is, "How is it going?" The response usually reflects their outer world. The second question to ask may be, "How's your spiritual life doing?" That's the heart of the matter.[4]

A middle-aged business man said, "I'll tell you what I struggle with, and it's constant. It's work vs. family vs. what I have left over for some of my own needs. How do I balance my life so it's not totally structured and rigid or totally hang loose and spontaneous? I like to achieve, but I also like to be with people and invest in them. So how do I achieve both?"

That's a good question. Perhaps what this man is really asking is, "How do I set priorities that work for me?"

Setting Priorities that Work

Many authors have written about setting priorities. As I waded through a multitude of books about organization and time management, I found that some were so detailed and complicated that I knew they wouldn't help. To follow them would add more clutter. Others did offer help, but often it was only bits and pieces that might make a significant difference. The authors of *Lifebalance* have some suggestions that make sense to me—and I hope to you.

But before you read on, remember this: *Reading about balancing your life won't balance it.* Wishing it were different *won't* make it happen. Trying won't bring about change. Giving up after several completed attempts won't do it. You may even wonder if balancing your life will give you the life you've always wanted. Give it a chance! Change will happen only if you're committed to following through for at least a month. That's right, a month. Then you'll be able to determine whether or not the change has made a difference in your life. It will also give you an opportunity to make any course corrections along the way. At the end of 30 days (and not before), take time to evaluate.

1. *List your priorities.* Perhaps the best place to begin is to list your present priorities. What are they? What you say they are *verbally* and what you say they are *behaviorally* could be totally different. But inwardly, what are they? For most of us, our priorities include some combination of people priorities (family, friends, God, coworkers, neighbors, ourselves), activity priorities (work, ministry, leisure, relationship building, exercising), and spiritual priorities (worship, service, learning). As you think about these options and more, make your personalized list of priorities. Don't worry about prioritizing the priorities at this point. The goal is to make as complete a list as possible.

People Priorities	Activity Priorities	Spiritual Priorities

Once you've made your list, think about what things are more important than others. Remember what we said before: Our list of the priorities we *say* we have may be different from our list of the priorities we *act out*.

2. *Do the most important thing first.* Has anyone ever given you a signed, blank check with a note instructing you to fill in any amount and cash it for yourself? Probably not. But it happened to Ivy Lee. When Charles Schwab was president of Bethlehem Steel, he told consultant Ivy Lee that if Lee could show him a way to get more things done with his time, he would pay Lee any amount of money within reason. Lee told Schwab that within 20 minutes he would give him an idea that would increase his output by at least 50 percent.

Lee gave Schwab a blank piece of paper and told him to do two things: Write a list of the six most important tasks that he had to do the next day, and number the tasks in order of their importance. Lee told Schwab to put the paper in his pocket, look at it the first thing the next morning, and work on the first task until it was finished. Lee further instructed Schwab that when he finished task one, he was to work on task two until it was done, and so on. It was all right if Schwab didn't complete all six tasks. Lee told him to try this system every day, and when he was convinced of what it could accomplish, he was to teach it to other people in the company. Lee's final words were to try the method as long as Schwab wanted and then send him a check for what Schwab thought the method was worth.

Several weeks later Lee received a $25,000 check along with a note saying that Lee's advice was the best Schwab had ever received. And it was. The advice helped Charles Schwab earn 100 million dollars and make Bethlehem Steel the largest independent steel producer in the world.[5]

3. *Find a balance.* In my counseling practice I've worked with

a number of people who were trying first of all to identify their priorities and then to commit to doing the most important thing first. Many of them had never done this before. The next step was to create the balance. Very often people ask the wrong question at this point. They ask, "What do I have to do?" But the most important questions may be these:

- What do I *choose* to do today?
- What would be *best* to do today?
- What do I *want* to do today?
- What would *glorify God* the most in what I choose to do?

The last question brings together the fact that we must rely on God while still making our own decisions. We belong to God, and he gives us freedom. What we do each day matters to him and could draw others to consider him. All these questions should be answered before you look at the absolutes of what must happen each day. As you ask that final question, also recite the following verses:

> "For I know the plans I have for you," says the LORD. "They are plans for good and not for disaster, to give you a future and a hope" (Jeremiah 29:11).

> Call to Me, and I will answer you, and show you great and mighty things, which you do not know (Jeremiah 33:3 NKJV).

Believing God's faithful, trustworthy promises will give you hope as you balance your life, and this is the way you'll discover the life you've always wanted. Let God be the leader.

Balanced Attitudes

We also need a second area of balance. Some call it "attitude" balance, although in many ways it reflects a personality balance. To

prioritize can mean downsizing rather than building up, casting off
rather than adding on. The key questions here are

- Will it matter in ten years?
- What do I need more of in my life?
- What do I need less of?
- How can I make this simpler?

When we learn to ask these questions consistently, we will also
develop the skill of *discretionary neglect*. This means we will develop
the skill of saying no, which is the skill of deciding what not to
do. The term *discretionary neglect* is especially important for the
people who are accumulators, the perfectionists, and the overly
structured.

How do these questions strike you? For some they're bothersome because they may challenge belief systems. For others they're
a breath of fresh air because people have been looking for this possibility for years. Can you imagine asking yourself these questions
each day…or even several times a day?

If you have trees, flowers, or hedges in your yard, you've probably had to do some trimming. Picture your life like an untrimmed
hedge. Where do you need to cut? Where will it be the most difficult? There are two ways of trimming. You can attack a hedge and
slash away…and it ends up looking botched. I've seen lives like that,
botched and chaotic. There was no planning involved in trying to
simplify; people just hacked and trimmed. The end result left much
to be desired. The better way is to figure out something you're cur-
rently trying to accomplish. It could be something specific like reor-
ganizing your garage or losing 50 pounds or becoming a parent
who disciplines without yelling. Then figure out what it will take to
reach your specific goal and nothing less than that goal. What type

of knowledge, skill, time, money, and cooperation from others will you need? I've seen people who wanted to lose 50 pounds discover that, first of all, that much weight loss would be too much for their height. It couldn't be done in three months, and it would drastically affect the meals and eating habits of other family members.

In others words, you may find that achieving your goal is unrealistic, unreasonable, and unattainable. Too many people set themselves up for failure, beat themselves up, try harder because of their guilt, and end up complicating their lives with zero enjoyment. It's better to adjust your bottom line and discover what you can live with and feel good about.

Look for what you can do less of in your life, what you can learn to accept, and what you can live without. It's amazing to hear several weeks later from those who have made such adjustments. They tend to have the same response: "Life is much easier for me and everyone else. The clutter is gone. I wonder why I didn't make these changes sooner."

Balanced Expectations

A third area in which we need balance is our expectations. Our lives are often cluttered because we have incredibly unrealistic expectations of ourselves, of others, and of life itself. Often our "own expectations" have been created from a blending of other people's and society's expectations. To what degree is this evident in your life?

Most people make their decisions based on their values. We all have two sets of values: operational and deep. Operational values are what we want immediately, whereas deep values are what is important over the long haul. What values are involved in what you decide to do? What values affect whether your life is simple or complex?

Another way to tone down your expectations is to concentrate more on the *process* of what you do than on the *outcome*. When we find satisfaction in the process, we are much more accepting of the outcome, whatever that may be.

One important influence for many people is the direction that comes from their consciences. People who live by their consciences, especially those shaped by Scripture, don't usually fall into the urgency-addiction trap or base what they do on others' responses. Their lives are fulfilled because they're confident about who they are and what they do.[6] Think about it. Is this you?

If you want to move toward the life you've always wanted, don't try to emulate anyone else. What works for someone else probably won't work for you. You will need to develop a balance and rhythm that is right for you.

Discretionary neglect also can be important as you work toward balanced expectations. Sometimes we need to confront the standards and restraints other people place on us. Look at the priority list you made in this chapter. What priorities have you chosen, and what "priorities" have others chosen for you? One woman said, "I'm still doing things the way my parents told me I must. They were both driven workaholics and couldn't stand to see anyone not be like them. They've been dead for more than 15 years, but it's as if they reach out from the grave and direct me with their shoulds. I keep hearing their voices."

Living with the Shoulds and Oughts

Should is a word that creates so much difficulty for us. We live our lives by unreasonable "shoulds." Many "shoulds" are good.

We need the absolutes of Scripture, for example. But consider the unnecessary absolute statements that many live by. What are you doing because of statements such as "I must do" or "I should" or "I am supposed to" or "I ought to"?

Have you ever kept track of the statements that run your life? Most people who do are not just mildly surprised but often shocked. As one man put it, "I never knew that so much of what I did came from this inner regulator that kept spewing out these directions, shoulds, oughts, and musts. I'm a person who likes to be in control of his life, and it was disheartening to see how much I *was controlled.*"

If you do list your absolute statements, evaluate them so you can decide whether to keep letting them dictate your life. It's a simple cost–benefit analysis.

1. List the benefits of doing what you "should" or "ought."
2. List the drawbacks of doing what you "should" or "ought."
3. List the benefits of *not* doing what you "should" or "ought."
4. List the drawbacks of *not* doing what you "should" or "ought."

Each item you write is a consequence. It's either a cost or a benefit. As you analyze the benefits of doing or not doing these "shoulds," you'll discover something very important: What you *think* you should do may not be the best for you to do. And this gives you a choice. You can choose to follow through with your shoulds because to do so would be beneficial. Or you can choose not to follow through, which may offer even more benefits.

But keep in mind that the "should" and "ought" statements are automatic. To lessen their control over you, you may need some replacement words like "I can do" or "I choose to" or "I've made a commitment to." It may seem like a game of semantics, but it's a way of breaking the hold these statements have over you and moving toward a balanced life.[7]

Rhythm and Tempo

One last thought about balance. A balanced and fulfilled life has tempo. Many people's operating tempo is too fast. We need a natural, balanced tempo or rhythm. If you've ever watched a marathon bicycle race, you'll understand tempo. In a long-distance race, the riders have a rhythm or tempo they learn to use because with it they can ride longer and farther. If riders go too fast, they wear themselves out. But going too slow can dull their mental capabilities. They may get bored and feel like giving up. The goal is to find that perfect "in between."

How's your pace in life affecting you? How is it affecting the members of your family? Family members need to be aware of each other's rhythm or tempo and learn to work in harmony. In bike races, the rider at the front of the pack actually breaks the wind for the others, making it easier for the others to ride. If you've ever watched geese fly in formation, you've seen the same dynamic. The goose at the head of the V breaks the wind resistance for the geese following. The others "draft" behind. After a while the lead goose drops back, and another takes over. Now and then one goose exhausts itself and has to land to recover. The other geese don't ignore it and keep moving ahead (as some families do). And they don't prod the goose that needs rest, saying, "Get with it! Hurry up. You've got to get your act together" (as some families do). When a goose drops out, a couple of others also drop out and stay with the tired one until it's ready to move on. The geese are attuned to individual differences in each other, and they move quickly to support one another. Sometimes we try to push ourselves and others beyond our capabilities and theirs. We have some lessons to learn. Once again balance is needed. How is the balance in your life?

Time for Reflection

1. After reading this chapter, on what area would you like to work to achieve and maintain balance?

2. What is the first step you will take to find that balance?

3. List the top three priorities in your life today.

4. Write on a three-by-five card the following questions and read them aloud each day for a month.

   • What do I choose to do today?

   • What would be best to do today?

   • What do I want to do today?

   • What would glorify God the most in what I do today?

5. In what way can you practice discretionary neglect?

6. Each day keep track of your "I should" or "I must" statements. Go back in this chapter to the four questions on "shoulds" and "oughts" and answer them.

One Person's
Reflections on Life

- *If my life were balanced, I would feel…*more balanced. I would take time to relax and to explore hobbies. I would not feel so rushed, so pressured. I would be more tranquil and feel a greater freedom to do things just for fun.

- *To me a fulfilled life means…*not having constant pressures, having time margins so that if specific things come up and/or I run into people, I could give them the time and energy that I'd like. Also, a simple life means enjoying just the basic necessities—not feeling as if I need a home, clothes, or other possessions to impress others. Ultimately, it's valuing people more than things and trusting God to provide.

- *What keeps me from changing my life is…*a strong work ethic ingrained in me. I feel guilty if I am not always accomplishing something worthwhile. I have great difficulty saying no because I don't want to disappoint others.

- *If I were to balance my life, I would…*commit to less and say no more often when people ask me to be somewhere or help out in some area.

6

Overloaded and Driven

I sat in the waiting room of the doctor's office. Do you know what I was doing? You guessed it…waiting. It didn't bother me. At that point in my life, nothing seemed to bother me except the fact that nothing seemed to bother or excite me. I was just blah. I didn't have energy. I didn't have any desire to do what I enjoyed. I didn't even enjoy fishing!

When I saw the doctor and he completed my physical, he said, "Well, I can't find anything physically wrong with you. The best way I can describe what's going on is that it's as if you are a one-ton truck that has been doing the job of a two-ton truck. You don't need an overhaul, but you do need a major tune-up. So do nothing for the next six weeks."

How would you have responded to that news had you been the one on the receiving end? Would you have accepted it gratefully, thankful you had no major physical problems? Or would you have argued with the doctor and said, "It's impossible! I can't do that. I'm behind now. I don't have enough time as it is. I'm pulled in 20 directions, and you want me to back off?" Or would you have sighed in relief as I did almost 25 years ago and thought, *Someone has given me permission to slow down, rest, catch my breath, quit driving myself, and recover. What a relief.* Often we learn lessons the hard way—by experience. I had brought myself to burnout by continuing to press myself with no recovery time in between. I changed that pattern.

Overload

A chapter title in Gordon MacDonald's book *Ordering Your Private World* expresses what many of us feel: "Has anyone seen my time? I've misplaced it!" But sometimes what we see as misplaced time is really a matter of overload. We have so much to do in the available time. We try to do the job of a two-ton truck when we may only be a pickup truck! I've felt that way before. Under the gun and under pressure. Typically my response had been to speed up to accomplish more. But that didn't work. Then I learned to slow down. That worked! Sounds strange to do just the opposite of what's needed, doesn't it? When you slow down, you're able to relax, see an overview of what needs to be done, trim your expectations, and accomplish the accomplishable.

Why *do* we overload ourselves and take on too much?

- Overconfidence—"I can do all things" (We're a legend in our own mind!)
- The need to achieve
- The need to avoid painful feelings when we don't achieve
- Failure to delegate tasks and the authority to go with them. You may be more adept at doing things yourself. You may

think, *It will take them two hours to do the job, and I can do it in a half-hour.* But how many half-hours do you have?

- Unrealistic expectations about how much time some things take. The result is we end up accomplishing little.[1]

Disorganization

Another reason for our struggle with time is our inability to organize. *Disorganization* means different things to different people. What appears to be disorganization to some people may be just a reflection of their personality. A cluttered desk for some people may be a symptom of disorganization, and yet to other people it's simply their style. In the midst of clutter they know where everything is!

What are the signs that your life is disorganized? Have you identified them? Do any of these examples hit home?

Your work area looks like it's either been ransacked or hit by a bomb. Uncompleted tasks that need to be done (no option on these) continue to accumulate, gather dust, grow mold, and just lie there.

Your home and car, which must be maintained regularly, are beginning to deteriorate. Your feelings of self-worth are low. You don't feel as if you're contributing what you could or are used to doing. It's not a matter of expecting too much either; it's knowing that you're functioning below par.

Forgetfulness seeps into your life. It could be telephone messages you forgot to return, a missed appointment, a missed deadline, a child left at school, a failure to remember your spouse's birthday. For me one of the worst and most embarrassing experiences as a marriage counselor is either to forget a client's appointment or (and this has happened) to walk into my waiting room and see two different clients both waiting for their eleven o'clock appointment. I double-booked! That's not the usual me. When your normal pattern of functioning becomes dysfunctional, it probably means you're overloaded and possibly disorganized.

Disorganization tends to foster "busyness." Our energy is invested in tasks that are not important. Getting something done is better than getting nothing done. When we do nothing, we end up daydreaming, avoiding necessary decisions, and procrastinating. How many times can you check for mail or phone messages, flip on the Internet, or sharpen pencils?

Disorganization can threaten your relationships with friends, with family members, and even with God. You have good intentions, but you're unable to follow through because of disorganization. Sporadic attempts to build an ongoing relationship with others dissolve to nothing. Being unorganized means some people lack the consistency to maintain quality relationships.[2]

Loss of Control

One of the by-products of leading a cluttered and overloaded life is feeling as if you've lost control. Actually you feel as if you've lost control of the events as well as time. But is that so unusual? Do we really have that much control over events and time? We may think we do or feel we must. But do we? A diagram Hyrum Smith uses in his book *The 10 Natural Laws of Successful Time and Life Management* gives a new perspective on control.[3]

No Control   Total Control

The left side represents events over which we have no control whatsoever, while the right side shows events over which we have total control. All the events in between are those over which we have partial control.

For many of us, feeling as if we have no control is a scary thing. To solve the problem, we do everything we can to gain more control, only to come back to the obvious truth: *Most of life is made up of events over which we have only partial control.*

The problem is not that things are out of our control; that is just part of life on earth. The real problem is our *response* to the things we can't control completely.

Do we fight, doggedly insisting that we *will* get this thing under control? Some individuals are control freaks. They believe they have to control everything.

Do we give up and just let life happen to us? There are some who believe they have no control and they couldn't care less. They just go with the flow.

Or do we accept that we can't control everything and learn to adapt? People who are able to live a balanced and uncluttered life have learned how to adapt. "Blessed are the flexible, for they will be less stressed."

If lack of control is a struggle for you, make a list of the personal and business situations over which you think you have total control. Indicate how much control you actually have by rating each item on the list from 1 to 5, with 5 representing total control. One man made the following list:

What I want to eat at home	4
When I get up in the morning	5
My wardrobe	5

The drive to work	3
Traffic	1
My dog	4
My cat	-1
Where I worship	5
My teenage son and what he wears	2
My wife's housekeeping	1
How my business is doing	1
Taxes	1

As the man progressed with his list, he decided to keep it for a week and add to it daily. By the end of the week he had quite an extensive list and a better feel for what he could control, what he couldn't control, and how to use his energy more effectively.[4]

Drivenness

Perhaps you'll identify with part or even all of this person's story. I've heard it often from men and women alike. Is this you?

I'm like many other people I know. You'd probably call me successful. That's true, at least in some ways. I'm what you call an overachiever. I get the job done, and I do it very well. I can't rest until it's complete.

There's so much to do that I feel as if I'm carrying a load. I'll admit I'm ambitious. And I do succeed. But I sometimes question whether I really deserve it. I wonder if I'm really capable or just lucky. I think I live my life based on fear. I'm afraid of not measuring up. I'm afraid that others will find out what goes on inside me. I'm afraid of letting down and having others wonder *What's wrong with you?* I want to be successful all the time. No, I *need* to be successful. So I keep doing more and enjoying less. I drive myself. It seems to be the only way to get it all done. Or is it? I wonder.

Do you drive yourself? Do you feel like a car that someone else is driving and you're in the fast lane with the accelerator pressed to the floorboard? If so, is this the life you've always wanted?

A middle-aged mother of three children said, "I've finally figured out what I am—a citrus fruit. In fact, a very specific kind—an orange. I feel as if I'm constantly being squeezed until there isn't one drop left in me. Some days I feel as if someone is scraping away at my rind! I don't ever have time or energy to think about adjusting my life. It's just one more thing to do!" Have you ever felt squeezed? The apostle Paul understands that squeeze, and he warns us against letting it happen: "Don't let the world around you squeeze you into its own mould" (Romans 12:2 Phillips).

Living a simple, balanced life means living a countercultural lifestyle. There's no other way to express it. A squeezed lifestyle is usually a driven, stressed life. A squeezed life means that we're allowing ourselves to be controlled or overloaded by someone or something else. We're not in control of a squeezed life, no matter how much we think we are.

Some people actually want to be driven people. They say, "Well, what's wrong with being driven? Show me those who aren't, and I'll show you people who are shirking their responsibilities. They're coasting through life." Driven people are found in every age group. We find them in baby busters, baby boomers, in-betweens, and traditionals.

Let me tell you about Jim, who's a reflection of many of us. Jim is driven. He finds his satisfaction through his achievements. He learned how to feel good about himself through accomplishments. It's been his way of finding love, acceptance, and approval. Once this pattern began, it accelerated, and he was on the fast track to success.

As Jim moves through life, he seems to accelerate his pace of searching for more and newer ways to accomplish things. And Jim has learned to do more than one thing at a time. Someone described him as "a blur of a person rushing by with an overflowing briefcase, dictating into a recorder, checking the time as he munches on a Big Mac." Often he's seen as intense, energetic, and competitive.

Oh, he enjoys what he does! He wakes up in the morning and can't wait to get started. Jim drives himself and competes with others. He often works 70 to 80 hours a week, and sees it as a badge of success. He often compares his number of work hours per week with other colleagues', as if he's in a competition. He does have some strong self-doubts, but you wouldn't suspect this by looking at him. He covers it well.

He suspects that he's inadequate, so he works hard to compensate. As someone said, "He trades sweat for talent." Jim thinks that the way to overcome this is to do more. So he prefers work to leisure. He has little use for free time and prefers weekdays to weekends. He can work anytime and anywhere. He takes no holiday or vacation. His home is a branch office, an extension of his profession. He makes the most of his time. Saving time is a goal. He rarely sleeps, and when he stops to eat, it's merely to feed his body, not to socialize. He makes schedules well in advance, punches the walk button several times at street corners, and plans, plans, plans.

Finally, he blurs the distinction between work and pleasure.

It's exhausting just reading about Jim! But there are plenty of Jims around. You may know some of them. They may be your boss or your coworkers. They may be your family members. They may be your friends.

Maybe you're like Jim.

Jim, like other driven people, has tunnel vision when it comes to life. Life is measured in results. That's the bottom line. The process doesn't count. It's what's at the end of the journey that counts. Perhaps you've been on a vacation with people like Jim. They get into the car, take off, and blaze across the country as fast as possible to "get there." You almost have to get a federal court order to stop at a restroom.

In *Lifebalance,* Richard Eyre describes a trip he took with his son:

> I took my young son on a hike one rare day. I knew it was important to be together, and he was excited. There was a plateau I figured we would climb to so we would have a level place to camp.
>
> The first part of the hike was great. We talked. We enjoyed being together. But we weren't moving very fast. I started pushing him to walk faster. I got a little upset at our slow pace. I finally found myself carrying his pack and almost dragging him.
>
> We made it to the plateau just in time to set up camp before dark. My boy fell asleep before I had the campfire going. When the flames grew and hit his face, I saw tear stains.
>
> I realized that there are always two goals. One is to get there. The other is to enjoy the journey. Too much emphasis on one can ruin the other.[5]

Driven people have been squeezed into living for the outward symbols of accomplishment: what vehicle they drive, what section of town they live in, the location of the office building in which they work, their job title, and even the social status of their church. Driven people are out of control. Enough is never enough. There always has to be more. They are never satisfied with what they produce, even if what they produce is for a good cause.

Charles Stanley, one of the best-known ministers of our time, described a time when he was physically exhausted but didn't want to slow down. So his doctor put him in the hospital, and his deacons wouldn't allow him to preach for three months! He finally gave in. He and his son went to a small island for five weeks. They talked, swam, fished, studied, and prayed. This is what Charles Stanley said about that experience.

> It sounds idyllic.
>
> When you've been running as fast as you can, however, and you are feeling driven twenty-four hours a day, getting off to an isolated place like that is a shock. Suddenly there's nothing to drive toward. There's nobody to get up for or to keep you going. It was like hitting a wall.
>
> I also felt so drained that I wondered if I'd ever regain sufficient strength to function normally. I had lots of self-doubts to go along with the exhaustion.
>
> I had no difficulty talking to God, and I certainly didn't place any blame on Him for the situation I was in. I knew that the problem was resident in me. I was feeling driven to succeed. I was committed to so many things, and I didn't know where to get off the wheel that was spinning. I wanted to stop wearing myself out, but I didn't know how to stop doing all that I was doing. I had a sense that I needed to stop overextending myself, but at the same time, I didn't know which activity to drop.
>
> Ultimately, I didn't want to give anything up. I wanted to do everything I was doing. I wanted to achieve everything I was achieving. I'd look at a situation and say to myself,

"Well, this is working—so why give that up?" And so it went for everything I was doing.

I don't know why I felt I had to do so much. Perhaps I was trying to prove to myself that I could do everything in which I was involved. Perhaps I was responding to the approval I was receiving. Perhaps it was related to the circumstances facing me in the church at that time.

I had a strong desire to see souls saved and to see the pews of the church filled with people. I had an equally strong desire to make sure that all of the programs at the church functioned to serve the people. I had big goals in lots of areas. I kept my goals continually in front of me. Short range. Middle range. Long range. I had them all lined up, and I was committed to making them happen, do or die. I had a strong desire to reach those goals as quickly as possible, but I had too little help. When you have that combination, the tendency is to spread yourself very thin and to become overextended, I had done just that.

The number one person who was driving me was me![6]

Are you overextended? If you had to evaluate your own overextension on a scale of 1 to 5, with 5 representing extreme overextension, where would you be?

Facing the Consequences

We can't live as driven, overloaded people without it costing us. Reflecting on some of the characteristics of driven people may help us determine whether or not we are willing to pay the price.

1. *Driven people often drift away from their inner values.* When we begin to follow the voices that lure us into the drive for success and achievement, we often silence the inner voice that tells us to

slow down, to stay in balance, to spend more time in serving than in chasing success, to keep our focus on God's call in our lives. Once the inner voices are muffled, it doesn't take much for us to start to compromise things that are important to us. Our drivenness may lead us into subtle patterns of deception. And we don't have the life we've always wanted.

2. *Driven people have a struggle with maintaining integrity.* If we lose touch with our inner values, we also run the risk of losing our integrity. Do you know what this word means? *Integrity* means to be "sound, complete, without blemish, crack, or defect." In the construction business, integrity refers to building standards that ensure the building will be safe. A building with integrity has to be properly designed, comply with all the building codes, be safe, and be able to function in accordance with its purpose.

When we say certain people have integrity, we mean that who they are on the outside is a true reflection of who they are on the inside. They're the same, through and through. We never have to doubt what they say or do because we know their actions and behaviors are in harmony with their inner values.

Integrity pleases God. Several passages in Scripture speak about integrity.

> I know, my God, that you examine our hearts and rejoice when you find integrity there. You know I have done all this with good motives (1 Chronicles 29:17).

> The integrity of the upright guides them, but the unfaithful are destroyed by their duplicity (Proverbs 11:3 NIV).

> People with integrity have firm footing, but those
> who follow crooked paths will slip and fall (Proverbs
> 10:9).

Consider your own life. If you had to evaluate your integrity on a scale from 1 to 5, with 5 representing high integrity, where would you be?

3. *Driven people have underdeveloped relational skills.* They have the potential to have meaningful relationships, but their commitment to the task or project often takes priority. Driven people usually have complicated rather than simple lives, and they can make it difficult for others to have simple lives.

The good news is that driven people get things done. But at what cost? In *Ordering Your Private World,* Gordon MacDonald wrote a very graphic portrayal of the problem.

> There is usually a "trail of bodies" in the wake of
> the driven person. Where once others praised him
> for his seemingly great leadership, there soon appears
> a steady increase in frustration and hostility, as they
> see that the driven person cares very little about the
> health and growth of human beings. It becomes
> apparent that there is a non-negotiable agenda, and
> it is supreme above all other things. Colleagues and
> subordinates in the orbit of the driven person slowly
> drop away, one after another, exhausted, exploited
> and disillusioned. Of this person we are most likely to
> find ourselves saying, "He is miserable to work with,
> but he certainly gets things done."
>
> And therein lies the rub. He gets things done, but
> he may destroy people in the process. Not an attrac-
> tive sight.[7]

4. *Driven people are competitive.* Everything in life fits into a win–lose contest. Winning makes driven people feel and look good. A win validates the need they have to feel they're important, valued, correct, and worthwhile. Sometimes we see this tendency in school settings. Not only do certain students want A's, but they want the top A in the class. And the greater the range between their score and the next one, the better they feel.

5. *Driven people often smolder with anger.* People focused on getting the job done are often wound so tight and are so intent on reaching their goal that if anything threatens their success, they erupt in anger. Sometimes they're angry because they realize they can't live up to their own standards.

6. *Driven people are overly busy.* They're on a treadmill to nowhere. Rarely do they think they've accomplished enough, so they drive themselves to do more. Unfortunately, they receive reinforcement from others: "You're amazing. You do so much, and you're always on the go." People on overdrive let others know about their bursting schedules. They may complain about what they do, but they like it. Busyness is a substitute (as well as an escape) for personal relationships. With their friends (if they have any) they're too busy even to discuss who they really are.[8]

We all hope and pray that we won't have to work for such people…or be married to one! Driven people can destroy themselves as well as others.

Over a hundred years ago a man named Cloris Chappell used to tell the story about two of the large steamboats that journeyed up and down the Mississippi River. Both boats left Memphis about the same time, going downriver to New Orleans. Since the boats were traveling close together, side by side, a friendly rivalry developed between the crews. They made comments about how slow the other boat was, and soon one crew challenged the other to a race.

One of the steamboats began to fall behind. It was running low on fuel. The crew had enough coal for the trip but not enough to race. As the boat fell farther and farther behind, one of the crew members grabbed some of the boat's cargo and threw it into the furnace. When they saw it worked as well as coal, they took the material they were supposed to transport to New Orleans and burned it. They succeeded in winning the race, but they burned their cargo.

We may accomplish all that we set out to accomplish, but who and what have we burned in the meantime? Usually it's ourselves. Someone said that driven people become burned-out people, who become dropped-out people.[9]

Driven people miss out on the life they've always wanted.

Antidotes to Disorganization and Drivenness

Have any of the symptoms of disorganization and drivenness cropped up in your life? Are you beginning to lean in that direction? What are you willing to do about it? You can begin by wanting to change and believing that it's possible. Then take one small step, and concentrate on what you *do* accomplish rather than what you don't.

Driven, burned-out people lack fun in their lives. What's fun for you? Yes, I know that fun is important for children, but whoever said that when we reach adulthood, fun and play have to stop? What do you enjoy? You're the one who determines what is fun for you. You may end up doing what your spouse or children want to do. You may like it somewhat because the others do, but when do you get to do what *you* enjoy?

Fun and enjoyment don't have to consume enormous amounts

of time. Many people limit their fun and enjoyment because their idea of fun is a three-week getaway. Why put all your enjoyment into a once-a-year event? I encourage you to think about enjoyment on a daily basis. This is a proven antidote for driven, overloaded, and burned-out people. It's one of the ways to get the life you've always wanted.

Do you believe you must always finish your work first and then you can play. That is unrealistic. Once again, the key is balance. You need work *and* play. Take a few minutes and identify what's fun for you, but do it in a different way. Make your list in columns based on how much time each activity takes.

Microbreaks 2-5 min.	Minibreaks 5-30 min.	Mellowbreaks 30 min.-2 hrs	Maxibreaks 2-12 hrs.	Megabreaks 1/2 day or more

You may be hesitant to list what you don't have time to do at the present. Don't limit yourself. You may want to read a book, but to get a solid stretch of 30 minutes seems impossible. That's all right. I've read novels in 15 to 20 minute segments a day, and sometimes that is done a minute or two at a time while I'm waiting for someone or something. It can be done.

You may have items that fit in just one category or some that could fit in all five. For example, I could list fishing in every column, reading novels in three, and so forth. You may want to make compiling this list a project for several days as different ideas come to you. Get yourself into the mode of reflecting about fun and play in your life.

Once you've completed your list, total up the number of items in each column. What do the numbers tell you about the fun in your life? The final step is to select one item from each column and determine when and how you will do it. Even on the days you are most rushed, stressed, overwhelmed, and overloaded, taking several microbreaks will do wonders for your energy level and attitude.[10]

Finding Your True Purpose

Disorganization and drivenness can have less power over you when you understand what your purpose is in life. Why are you here? Do you know? When this question is settled, it eliminates your inner feelings of choice and confusion. It brings a peace that enables you to move forward. God's Word says, "You created everything, and it is for your pleasure that they exist and were created" (Revelation 4:11). "The Lord takes pleasure in his people" (Psalm 149:4 TEV).

Rick Warren, in *The Purpose-Driven Life,* says:

> You were planned for God's pleasure. The moment you were born into the world, God was there as an unseen witness, *smiling* at your birth. He wanted you alive, and your arrival gave him great pleasure. God did not *need* to create you, but he *chose* to create you for his own enjoyment. You exist for his benefit, his glory, his purpose, and his delight.

Bringing enjoyment to God, living for his pleasure, is the first purpose of your life. When you fully
understand this truth, you will never again have a
problem with feeling insignificant. It proves your
worth. If you are *that* important to God, and he con-
siders you valuable enough to keep with him for eter-
nity, what greater significance could you have? You
are a child of God, and you bring pleasure to God
like nothing else he has ever created.[11]

I remember hearing a pastor share how he and another man had
been exhausted after ministering together in Moscow for several
days. But as they were leaving, the pastor turned to his friend and
with excitement in his voice said, "Isn't this great? We were born for
this!" He knew what he was supposed to be doing.

What were *you* born for? Have you ever thought about it or discussed it with anyone? The Westminster Catechism asks, "What is
the chief end of man?" The answer is this: "The chief end of man is
to glorify God and to enjoy Him forever." That sounds good, but
what does it mean for you personally? And how do you do this?

If you understand and work toward your purpose and your
mission, when you come to the end of your life you can look
back and say, "Mission accomplished." You lived for the purpose
for which you were intended. Are you living for God's pleasure?
Disorganization diminishes when you make this discovery. It also
vanishes when you're able to stand outside of yourself and say,
"These are my assets and strengths. And these are my limitations.
I'll use my strengths in the areas where they can best be used and
give it my all. I'll also not try to move into areas where I have little
or nothing to give. I'll admit that I can't do everything and that I
can't be everything to everyone." People who take on tasks that are

outside their abilities or that are not suited for their personality strengths soon begin to disintegrate.

It's all right to say "I can't do that because I don't have the ability" and "I'm not really interested in doing that." Others will try to pressure you into areas that you couldn't care less about. Not everyone wants to be a computer whiz or know how to evaluate the stock market or become a distributor for XYZ products or become proficient at fly-fishing. Sometimes we allow the misplaced enthusiasm or bias of others to move us in directions we really don't care to go. But we operate on the myth that "refusal equals rudeness." We have not learned the fine art of the gracious no.

As you learn your unique purpose and mission, you will be in a better position to curtail the drivenness and disorganization in your life. And you'll begin to experience life the way you—and God—want.

Time for Reflection

1. In what areas do you feel disorganized? What will you do about it?

2. How does your organization or lack of it contribute or hinder a simplified lifestyle?

3. Over what do you have control in your life? In what area should you learn to let go?

4. To what degree are you driven? What can you do to be less driven?

5. How would finding your life's purpose help you simplify your life? What steps can you take to find your purpose or to further your purpose?

One Person's
Reflections on Life

- *If my life were balanced, I would feel...* less pressure to do things. I would be less driven and would be content in my circumstances because my eyes are on the Father and not on events or circumstances.

- *To me a fulfilled life means...* taking the time to appreciate the little things, such as watching sunsets or smelling the roses. But it's not so much an outward lifestyle as it is an inner experience of deep relationship with the Lord.

- *What keeps me from changing my life is...* my lack of discipline. I hate to admit this, but it's true.

- *If I were to have the life I always wanted, I would...* prioritize all the things I am involved with and then pray over the list. I would then get rid of the things that are low priorities and narrow my focus and efforts to a specific area/priority. Also I would say no more often. That would feel good!

7

Energy Drainers and Energy Boosters

Several years ago a friend and I went fishing at Upper Twin Lake near Bridgeport, California. It was a beautiful spot at the foot of some of the High Sierra Mountains. The fish were practically jumping into our boat. I don't remember how many we caught and released.

Then a cloud blew in, and a heavy rainstorm drove us from the lake. But being diehard fishermen and not wanting to miss the frantic bites, we pulled our car up right next to the lake. We cast out as far as we could and then sat in the car with the windows partially open and the rods sticking out. People drove by just shaking their heads.

Finally the rain let up, and we headed back to our boat. There were about twenty rental boats lined up next to each other at the dock. Each one had about six inches of water in it. I told my friend that if he would bring back the fishing gear from the car, I would bail out the boat. He agreed.

When my friend returned with the poles, he stood watching me. Several other people stood around watching and smiling. I bailed and bailed, working as hard and fast as I could. It was almost dry in the boat. Then Marv said, "Norm, you're doing a great job. The only problem I see is this ain't our boat!"

I stopped, looked up at him, and exclaimed, "What?" I looked at the boat number and realized he was right!

"But the folks who belong to that boat sure want to thank you for bailing it out!" he added as he chuckled. After all that hard work, I was drained of energy. I'd spent it on the wrong boat.

Sometimes the reason we aren't getting anywhere for all of our efforts is that we're spending the energy on the wrong beliefs about what it will take to make our lives different. The things we do to change our lives may actually drain our energy rather than give us energy. Let's look at some beliefs to determine whether they may be draining us.

Energy-Draining Beliefs

Some people believe "the harder you work or the more you sweat, the more you'll get." Are results directly related to how hard you work? Many people work hard and still do not change. They end up being driven, and working consumes their lives.

Some people believe "activity means productivity." I've seen active, intense hamsters running inside a cage, but they're running around in circles. Activity cannot replace results. The busiest beaver may be working but not always productive. I've heard many say, "What did I accomplish? I was busy all day, but I don't have anything to show for it."

Recently a friend in a high administrative position told me, "I spend the first two hours every day answering e-mail. I accomplished more and felt more productive before I was hooked up to the computer. I feel as if I'm doing things other people ought to be doing."

Some people believe "efficiency means effectiveness." Remember that when you're *efficient,* you do the job *right;* when you are *effective,* you do the *right job.* Which do you think is more important? Activities don't take the place of having a goal and using your time to achieve it. Effectiveness has to come before efficiency.

Some believe "to get ahead, you *must* burn the midnight oil." If you believe this, you're on the road to a new career—becoming a career workaholic. This is costly to you and your family. It's a fast track to burnout and disaster.

Some believe "the best way to do something is the easiest way." These individuals stop at the first sign of an obstacle, time commitment, or effort. They usually end up with results proportionate to their effort. Changing a life takes effort. There's nothing easy about making your life a bit easier.

Some believe "work is work. There's no enjoyment to it." Sometimes work is fun and enjoyable; sometimes it's not. I've always enjoyed work even though there have been difficult times. Those who have learned to enjoy even the most mundane job have done so through their attitude. And this comes through seeing work as a way to glorify God.

Some believe "there is only one way to do things." The more rigid and inflexible we grow, the more stagnant we become. This stagnation can lead to mediocrity.

Some believe "I work best under pressure." This may be true at times, but consider this: The pressure that some people seem to need may be overwhelming to others. Some use this belief to justify their procrastination.

Maybe you have been operating under one or more of these

energy-draining beliefs.[1] If so, is your belief helping you attain the life you want?

The Superman or Superwoman Syndrome

Perhaps one of the most damaging energy-draining beliefs we hold is that the best way to get something done is to do it our-selves. One of my favorite comic-book heroes was Superman. You know the story. Superman's parents sent him to Earth in a strange-looking spaceship because his planet was about to be destroyed. So Superman ended up in a Midwest pasture and was found by a farm couple.

Superman grew up as Clark Kent, who became a mild-mannered reporter. But when he changed into Superman, he could leap over the tallest building and stop a bullet in midair. Superman came out of hiding only when he needed to help others.

Did you ever notice some of the other features about him? I never saw him spill food on his clothes or trip on a sidewalk. His clothes fit perfectly, and he never seemed to perspire. He handled every problem by himself. *Not once did he ever ask for help.* Not once.

When I was younger, I thought there was only one Superman. But as I grew older, I began to discover many of his clones. Like Superman, these people never asked for help. Do you? Do you attempt to do it all and be all things to everyone? If so, your life isn't fulfilling. It's supercomplicated. If you suffer from Superman or Superwoman syndrome, you collect activities as well as being a master juggler. You're fueled by accolades of praise: "I don't know how you do so much." You love to fly from one rescue operation to the next. You're everyone's helper, everyone's solution, the one who bails everyone out. You rarely take off your supercape. You end up being everyone's hero or heroine.

The feelings of being needed, well liked, and admired are great. But superpeople have lost the sense of balance that must accompany those feelings. They've lost touch with their own needs and concerns. And, unlike Superman, these superpeople run out of energy; their fuel source runs low. One day they wake up and feel like Superman when he encounters a piece of Kryptonite from his old planet—weakened and immobilized.

If you suspect you suffer from Superman or Superwoman syndrome, consider these questions:

- Do you feel you rarely have any time just for you?
- Do you find it hard to say no to other people's needs?
- Are you a problem solver for others?
- Is *delegation* a word that's foreign to you?
- Are others constantly calling or asking you for something?
- Would you rather do things yourself or ask for help?
- Do you continue to improve on whatever you do?

If you relate to several of these, you may be trying to wear the supercape. And you know what? It doesn't fit you. It never will. People who try to be superpeople end up with very little pleasure in their lives. The rushing about and pushing themselves leads to an empty existence.[2] And it's certainly not a balanced, fulfilling life.

The Superman or Superwoman syndrome is not a loving or giving pattern of living; it's actually a selfish one. It denies others the opportunity to give, to share, to learn, to grow, and to develop. It stunts their growth. If you qualify for the syndrome, you need to make some changes. To restore balance and simplify your life, try the following:

- Learn to say no.
- Learn to encourage others.
- Learn to accept one request and automatically turn down the next. (Ouch.)
- Learn to ask others for help before they ask you.
- Learn to quit volunteering so much.
- Learn to become dependent.
- Learn to enjoy yourself for who you are rather than for what you do.
- Learn to depend upon God to direct and lead your life.

Energy depletion adds clutter to our lives even if our lives are already balanced. You can't accomplish even the basics if there isn't any energy.

Many people today describe their lives with the terms *depletion, running on fumes,* and *dragging.* Most of us recognize these. We've all felt this way or used these expressions when the fuel in our energy tank runs out. Many people run around each day with very little reserve in their tanks. Others seem to be always out of fuel and constantly tired.

How do *you* feel at the end of a day? Tired? Exhausted? Drained? And what happens to your life when your energy is gone? If you're like many people, your life becomes more cluttered. That's even more frustrating.

Maintaining Energy

How do people maintain their energy? First, they discover how they get energy or how they're energized. We're all different in our personality preferences. Some people are energized by being with other people. They like social or work environments where they interact with many others. They make phone calls and welcome the interruption of calls because it involves talking with others. Interacting with people recharges their batteries. But if they're cut off from people and are isolated, their energy starts to diminish. We call these people extroverts, and they make up about two-thirds of our population. Some of them are exhausted each day because of not having enough contact with people.

Others gain their energy from quiet times. They enjoy being alone, reading, or working by themselves. Being around too many people for too long a time drains their batteries. To recharge, they must have some quiet time. These are introverts. This is their personality bent. There is nothing wrong with being an introvert or an extrovert. But people of each type need to understand their own and others' unique energy drainers or energy boosters.

Take Lessons from Energetic Children

Perhaps you've seen people who seem to have an abundance of energy and rarely seem to run dry. I made an interesting discovery recently. Adults who are able to perform at such high levels of energy essentially follow the same thinking and behavior patterns that young children follow. Consider the following energy-gaining traits that are true of most children.

1. *Children search out activities that are fun to do.* Enjoyment and fun are high values for children. When they are doing something they enjoy, they seem to have boundless energy. What enjoyable experience have you had recently?

2. *Children are flexible.* Children can jump from one activity to

another, responding to what interests them the most. They are adaptable. In what ways are you flexible?

3. *Children are curious, investigative, and always willing to try something new.* When children's curiosity is aroused, they often become very excited and jump with glee. They're energized by discovery. Describe some event that you recently explored. Did it energize you?

4. *Children smile and laugh a lot.* Children know the wonderful release that comes from deep, contagious laughter. We all need to laugh a little. Better yet, we need to laugh a lot. Laughter is one of God's gifts. An Old Testament proverb reminds us, "A cheerful heart is good medicine, but a broken spirit saps a person's strength" (Proverbs 17:22). Laughter relieves tension. It brings balance into life. It gives respite from the heaviness of life's concerns and griefs. Are you known as someone who laughs a lot?

5. *Children experience and express emotions freely.* They let them out, often without any self-consciousness. It's only as we grow older that we learn to shut down. How freely do you express what you're feeling?

6. *Children are creative and innovative.* When you think of every problem as an opportunity and a challenge, you become more creative. In what area of life are you creative?

7. *Children keep moving.* They're physically active. Sometimes it's hard to keep up with their high level of energy. I've been exercising almost every day since 1981. Physical exercise is an energy booster. It's given me endurance and lowered my heart rate from 80 to 58 beats per minute. It also helps keep

my weight under control. What type of regular exercise program are you following?

8. *Children are constantly growing mentally and physically.* It's possible to learn new skills no matter what our ages. When we stop growing and learning mentally, we don't stay at the same level. We regress. What new physical skill have you learned in the last five years? How have you grown mentally in the past year?

9. *Children are willing to take risks.* They have little fear about staying at something they're not good at. They're not so afraid to fail. People who take risks have more chance of succeeding than those who won't take risks. Remember that the turtle makes progress only when it sticks its head out. We're no different. What is the last risk you took?

10. *Children listen to their bodies and rest when they need to.* Young children can go for hours with seemingly endless energy, but when their energy is spent, they collapse and sleep hard. I've had to learn the rhythm of rest. If I have a break at my counseling center and I'm tired, I take a ten-minute nap. If I'm writing at home in the afternoon and my eyelids begin to sag, I put down my pen, lean back, and doze for a few minutes. My body says I need it. I listen. Do you argue with your body or heed its messages?

11. *Children dream and imagine.* Why stop dreaming and imagining when you're 30 or 60 or 80? The older we become, the more we can combine our dreaming with wisdom. What dream can you pursue?

12. *Children seldom worry.* We often envy children because they seldom get bogged down with the cares of life. We adults,

however, can become immobilized by worry. The Scriptures have much to say about worry:

> Don't worry about anything; instead, pray about everything. Tell God what you need, and thank him for all he has done (Philippians 4:6).

> Worry weighs a person down; an encouraging word cheers a person up (Proverbs 12:25).

> All the days of the desponding afflicted are made evil [by anxious thoughts and forebodings], but he who has a glad heart has a continual feast [regardless of circumstances] (Proverbs 15:15 AMP, brackets in original).

> A glad heart makes a happy face; a broken heart crushes the spirit (Proverbs 15:13).

Remember that when you worry about the possibility of something happening, your worry doesn't prevent it. But it could help to bring it about. What are your worries? Are they worth holding on to?

In a poignant New Testament story, "Jesus called a little child to his side and set him on his feet in the middle of [all the people.] 'Believe me,' he said, 'unless you change your whole outlook and become like children you will never enter the kingdom of Heaven'" (Matthew 18:2-3 Phillips). Did you catch that phrase "change your whole outlook"? Jesus calls us to look at life through children's eyes. They see life as simple. Their faith is also simple. Is yours?[3]

Recharging Your Batteries

Most of our time during a day is focused on doing and giving out. It's only when our batteries run dry that we think of replenishment. If we understand that we will need energy boosters during the day, we can plan wisely to give ourselves the recharging we need. In major auto races the driver and his or her team plan out their pit stops in advance. Without careful planning, the car could run out of fuel and be out of the race permanently. Some days we end up feeling like the out-of-fuel car.

Everyone's metabolism and body needs are a bit different. But most people have several energy-draining or energy-boosting times of the day. Ann McGee-Cooper discusses four of these times in her informative book *You Don't Have to Go Home from Work Exhausted.* The four times are getting ready for your daily work, commuting to work, eating lunch, and commuting from work. While McGee-Cooper's insights are aimed primarily at people who work outside the home, I believe that her perceptions will also help those of us who do our work in our homes.

Getting Ready for the Day

During the next few days as you prepare for your day's work, think about what drains your energy and what might boost your energy. Are you a morning person? Do you prepare for your day in a quiet place with few distractions? Or do you get ready with several other people in your household? If some of those people are young children who need lots of help, your energy will drain pretty fast.

Do you take time to eat something that will give you energy or do you gulp a cup of coffee and then grab a fast-food, high-cholesterol breakfast? What's going on in your mind as you get ready for the day? This is a major arena of energy drain or infusion. Are you reviewing the day, or do you plan just to let it unfold? Here again, some people are proactive; some are reactive. Proactives respond to the events of the day from an inner foundation. Reactive people allow the day to happen and react to it as it comes. They allow events and people—even the weather—to determine how they respond and feel. If dark clouds fill the sky, they feel gloomy. Proactive people carry their own weather around with them.[4] Attitude, once again, makes a difference.

What do you think about? Do you worry about what could go wrong, what you may forget, or how you'll get all the work done? What do you listen to as you prepare for your day? Does it upset you or refresh you? Are your thoughts negative or positive? Are you patient or impatient?

Some couples and families energize each other in the morning by asking how they can pray for the others during the day. Knowing that someone will be praying for you gives you a more solid perspective of the day.

Many people find that their primary morning energizer is taking time for Scripture reading, worship, and prayer. Allowing the Lord to remind us that he is in control and that he will be with us throughout the day gives the day the best possible foundation.

Commuting

For those of you who work outside the home, the commute may be the greatest energy drain. I've heard several Christians say they lose their sanctification during their morning commute! Commuting can be taxing. If you drive to work, you know that traffic and delays get worse each day. It won't change. Expect the unexpected. Plan for it mentally. Leave early. Have music or instructional tapes in your car.

Some people I know take a bottle of bubble soap with them in the car. When the traffic grinds to a halt and they're impossibly stuck, they open the window and begin blowing bubbles. Crazy?

Yes! But they not only enjoy the time and get a lot of attention, they also help everyone around them relax. Use your commuting time to reflect on positive things:

- Think about how you will greet each person at work in a positive and perhaps new way.

- Rehearse what you plan to accomplish in the first hour.

- Reflect on what you want to go well today, and plan for it.

Resist using your time in the car for starting your workday early by phoning clients or colleagues. Try to see the commute as a buffer time between leaving home and setting foot in your workplace.

For those of you who live in metropolitan areas and take public transportation, use the time on the bus or train to read the newspaper or a compelling book. Or, if you're an extrovert, use the time to greet those who take the bus or train with you every day. Again, resist the temptation to see the bus or train as your "moving office," from which you make phone calls and set up meetings.

Taking Time for Lunch

The third key energy time of the day is the midday meal. Keep in mind that stress and food don't mix well. Whether you work in your home or outside your home, how you spend this mealtime has an impact on your energy. Do you take working lunches or relaxing lunches? Do you spend it with people or alone? If you spend it alone, do you work while you eat? If you spend time with other people, do you talk about pleasant things or do you rehash the morning's problems?

If you eat rich, high-fat foods for lunch, you know where your energy is going for the next two hours. The more energy that's diverted to processing your food, the less you have for work.

Coming Home

The final key energy time of the day is the transition from the workday to the evening. For people who work outside the home, this transition will be the commute home. For people whose work is done in the home, this transition is not as obvious. And that may cause a problem.

What's happened to your energy during the day will influence this transition. For instance, you may have used a lot of energy dealing with one of the following situations:

- People who constantly complain or gripe
- People who try to control you or others
- People who disregard your schedule
- People who express negative nonverbal signals, such as frowning, sighing, rolling their eyes, making demeaning sounds
- People who use anger and temper tantrums to get their way
- People who gossip
- People who block open communication and honest feelings
- People who do not respect your personal boundaries

If your workday has been affected by any of these energy drainers, the transition may be a stressful one.

If you work outside the home, make sure that when you leave your workplace, you leave it in every way—not just physically. Too often the mental and emotional aftereffects follow you home and interfere with the rest of your evening. If you work at home, create a transition activity that will help you separate the work part of your day from the rest of the day. This is particularly important for parents who have young children. Give yourself some breathing space, even if it is just a ten-minute break to read, before your children return from school, bursting with their needs and the aftereffects of their day.

Several people have devised creative ways of disengaging from their workplace. One man told me that before he leaves his office, he writes on a pad what he needs to do the next day so he doesn't have to carry it around in his mind. Another person walks around the block at various speeds just to get the circulation going for the drive home.

For those of you who commute, try to arrange for flexible scheduling so you can avoid traveling during rush hour.

Other people have found ways of using the transition time to prepare for the people who will be in their home when they arrive. A busy executive shared that when he gets into his car, he puts a gag rule on his thoughts and flips down the visor, which holds a picture of his family. He does this each day to remind himself of who now deserves his attention. A creative salesperson spends the time driving home creating new off-the-wall ways of greeting each of the four family members waiting for him at home. A friend always called home before he left the office. He and his wife discussed which of them had the greater need when he arrived home so they would both be prepared. Some days he needed to run in the park for 20 minutes before dinner, and some days she needed him to watch the kids so she could unwind. Knowing this in advance made the commute more relaxing.

Many use the commuting time to relax. Some find that listening to classical or Christian music is relaxing and energizing for them. Another person said she prayed for different drivers, making her feel as if she had a ministry that day.[5]

The Lord Renews My Strength

The best source of energy for each day is the Lord. He promises to give us strength. But how often do you talk to him or think about him? When the Scriptures say pray without ceasing, they're talking not about praying every minute of the day but about the reality that we can be in unceasing communication with God. Do you pray throughout the day? Do you reflect on his Word throughout the day? Do you go to him *before* you're out of energy? Reflect on these promises from God's Word:

> I love you, LORD; you are my strength. The LORD is my rock, my fortress, and my savior; my God is my rock, in whom I find protection. He is my shield, the strength of my salvation, and my stronghold (Psalm 18:1-2).
>
> The LORD is my strength, my shield from every danger. I trust in him with all my heart. He helps me, and my heart is filled with joy. I burst out in songs of thanksgiving (Psalm 28:7).
>
> He gives strength to the weary and increases the power of the weak (Isaiah 40:29 NIV).
>
> But those who wait on the LORD will find new strength. They will fly high on wings like eagles. They will run and not grow weary. They will walk and not faint (Isaiah 40:31).

Time for Reflection

1. What's the greatest energy drain in your life at this time?

2. What beliefs drain your energy?

3. Do you try to be a superperson? Who pays the price for that?

4. In what way are you like a child?

5. What energy boosters can you practice more often?

6. What key time of the day is the greatest energy drainer for you? What two steps can you take to boost your energy at those times?

One Person's
Reflections on Life

🕊 *If my life were energized, I would feel*...the strength that flows from a close relationship with God the Father, God the Son, and God the Holy Spirit. I would gain energy from leaving my problems in the Lord's hands.

🕊 *To me a fulfilled life means*...pushing back the activities and finding time to be close to God, to nature, and to the people who need to know they are loved.

🕊 *What keeps me from changing my life is*...the struggle to survive. Work consumes my hours. I need to retreat from the chaos and focus on beauty, music, books, an aesthetically pleasing environment. Spending time with people who are like-minded helps me to simplify my life.

🕊 *If I were to have the life I always wanted, I would*...retire to the mountains to enjoy the peace and tranquility of nature from sunrise to sunset. My focus would be on God's creation: the sun, moon, stars, clouds, rainbows, and changing seasons.

8

Downscaling Our Things

Downscaling and *downsizing* are common terms today. They can be positive and negative. Downsizing is positive for companies as they seek solutions for staying afloat in a competitive and cost-conscious environment.

Downsizing is negative for employees because it could mean they're next to be told that the company is too small to support their jobs. As "the survivor game" plays out across our country, it's created a survivor sickness similar to the psychological numbing of post-traumatic stress disorder, the disorder experienced by soldiers after their war experiences or by rescue workers after a disaster like the Oklahoma City bombing, the 9/11 tragedy, or Hurricane Katrina. The survivors of downsizing experience fatigue, resentment, fear of future, loss, and even guilt because they survived. Some survivors experience as much stress as those who were let go.[1]

But a new undercurrent of downscaling is happening in our country today, and it's purposeful. It's the trend of individuals and families toward developing a more relaxed, balanced, and fulfilled lifestyle. Many are moving from an emphasis on materialism and consumption to a focus on personal needs, families, and relationships.

More and more people are deciding to step off the fast track or steep career ladder. The continuous step up for more wealth, fame, and achievement hasn't led to the satisfaction they expected. It's been interesting to see how willing many professionals are to slow down their career progress in order to spend more time with their families. A survey of a thousand men and women indicated that four-fifths of the respondents said they would rather have a career path with flexible, full-time work hours and more available time with their families. They preferred slower career advancement to faster advancement and inflexible hours.[2]

What this trend says is that exhausted men and women are finding that something is missing from their "successful" lives.

Downscaling Our Possessions

Many of us have also decided we own too many things. We bought these "things" assuming they would make our lives more manageable and, somehow, simpler. But in the end the items made them more cluttered. Most people are surprised by the extra work many possessions add to their lives. I've watched a family purchase a boat with the goal of family togetherness and fun. Before they made the purchase, however, they forgot to ask an important question: What will it cost us—in time, money, and energy—to maintain it? The very purchase they thought would bring them enjoyment and togetherness ended up being a source of tension. It became hard to find a time when they could all go boating together or to agree on where they would go. They experienced disappointment when the family members who were supposed to clean up the boat didn't.

Ad campaigns tell us how much we need more stuff to fulfill our lives and make us "happy." We need campaigns to tell the ad campaigns that we don't believe what they're saying and that we won't buy into it. This means once again going against the voices of our culture. But in doing this we set ourselves free from the tyranny of those trying to tell us what is best for us. Tim Kimmel talks about this in *Surviving Life in the Fast Lane:*

> Keeping the average family discontent is vital to our economic system. In order to lure me to a particular product, an advertiser must create a dissatisfaction for what I have—or a nagging desire for what I don't need. In order to be content we must learn to discipline or control our desires. When people fail to discipline their desires, they feel incomplete. A gloomy cloud of inadequacy follows them around. It's difficult to maintain deep relationships with such people—their feelings of inadequacy drain your emotions. When people fail to control their desires, they give in to the powers in the world system that desire to control them.[3]

Times are changing. Businesses may not like it, but people will continue to spend less. We are past the decades of indulgence. For years the typical American was described as "a person who drives a bank-financed car on a bond-financed highway on credit-card gas to open a charge account at a department store so he can fill his savings-and-loan financed home with installment-purchased furniture."[4] With soaring gas prices our perspective on cars is changing, and our rising debt is finally getting our serious attention.

Take an Inventory of Your Possessions

What do you own? Or perhaps the question is, What owns you? This is an opportunity for you to evaluate your possessions. Photocopy the chart on the next page. You may need to make several copies to have space for all of your possessions.

In the column on the left-hand side of the chart, make a list of your possessions and major purchases. Be sure to list *every* item you own. It may help to go through each room of the house as you make your list. After you've completed this part, write down nontangible items you've purchased, such as education or vacations.

In the second column, indicate with a check mark why you own that particular item. Is it something you need, something for your happiness or fun, something for status, or something that makes you feel good about yourself? After you have completed this, go back and add the $ symbol next to each item for which you still owe money. That could even be a vacation or cruise you're still paying off.

Think of the fullest or happiest time of your life. It could be now, 5 years ago, or even 20 years ago. Place an X next to each item that you possessed at that time in your life. You may be surprised by what you discover.

In the very last column check off the things you believe you will own in the same form 15 years from now.[5]

What has the inventory taught you about your possessions? If you choose to downscale, where will you begin?

Possession Inventory						
List your possessions	Why do you own these things?				What did you own at your happiest time?	What will you possess 15 years from now?
	Need	Happiness	Status	Feel good about me		

Declutter Your Life

Part of downscaling is getting rid of the clutter in our lives. Clutter is anything that keeps us from being all we can be and having the life we always wanted. It's anything that distracts, creates detours in our lives, gets in our way, and makes our lives unnecessarily complicated. Clutter has the potential to leave us feeling out of control and victimized.

The statement "We might need this or use this *someday*" is a good clue that you probably won't ever use it. It may help to ask, "Do we see ourselves using this in the next year? In the next two years? The next five years?" If not, what does that say to you?

Accumulation is a sport for some people. The greater the drive to accumulate, the more complicated and cluttered life becomes!

Some people say, "Hey, I'm not materialistic. I'm not controlled by things. How could I be? I'm not wealthy!" You don't have to be wealthy to accumulate things. If your security is based on what you have, accumulation will occur. Your accumulation may be the result of garage sales and swap meets rather than sprees at Nordstrom's or Macy's. You've probably seen the bumper stickers that say, "The one who dies with the most toys wins" or "I shop until I drop." Perhaps we need one that says, "The one who accumulates the most owes the most."

In their book *Downscaling*, Dave and Kathy Babbitt comment on our consumer mentality:

> Shopping has become a national sport, with many participants and few spectators. Those who acquire the most possessions join the ranks of the prestigious in the winner's circle. Americans have made a pastime of consumption as entertainment. We have collected trivia that has become junk before it's even paid off.

From this trinket to that toy, things tend to be an end in themselves instead of a means to a more fulfilling way of life.

The basis for an unceasing acquisition of things is often a spirit of discontent, pride, insecurity, greed, rejection, or emptiness. When was the last time you bought something you really didn't need but felt compelled to buy in order to fill a different kind of need through your purchase? In the end, did it satisfy?

Did you ever consider that there may be a correlation between the accumulation of things and our frantic lifestyle? We are so used to buying whatever we want, even if only on a small scale, that denying ourselves seems unthinkable. The busier we are, the less time we have to consider creative alternatives. It is easier to plunk down dollars or a credit card as we rush to the next activity than to evaluate the necessity of our purchase.[6]

Usually the satisfaction from accumulation is short lived. Simplifying our lives often leads to some downscaling. Let me suggest that you conduct a clutter search of your life. The intent is slightly different than the inventory you just completed. Look at each room in your house. Ask yourself these questions: What things in this room complicate my life? How could changes in this room simplify my life? Make a list of your responses. Then do the same for the next room.

You may feel resistant to this idea. That's all right. You may feel as if somebody's meddling with your life. That's understandable. Is what you are doing with your life now complicating it or giving you the life you want? If it is, don't change. If not, you don't have that much to lose.

But how do you change? You start small.

Someone has suggested using a 10-percent plan in simplifying and downscaling your life. As you evaluate the clutter in your house, reduce your inventory by 10 percent. If you're not ready to part with certain items, that's all right. Just put them away, and at a later time decide whether you've missed them. If you haven't, what does that tell you?

Have you ever heard of the 80/20 principle? If not, it may have a profound impact on simplifying your life. This principle says that 80 percent of the value of things is usually concentrated in only 20 percent of the items. Think about it for a minute. How do restaurants know how much food to have on hand? It's because 80 percent of the meals ordered come from 20 percent of the items on the menu. It's the same for television. Eighty percent of programs watched come from 20 percent of the program line-up. Eighty percent of phone calls made come from 20 percent of the callers. And in many stores 80 percent of the dollar value of an inventory is once again found in 20 percent of the items.

If this holds true in other areas, take a look at what's in your cupboards, closets, and drawers. If 80 percent of the space is taken up by stuff that's used only 20 percent of the time, is it necessary?[7]

Over the years I've done a lot of counseling with people in grief. This involves helping people handle losses of all kinds, including loss of a job, a home, a marriage, a child, a parent. These losses happen *to* people; they were out of their control.

When you declutter your life, you may feel a sense of loss even though you're in charge of the process. The authors of *'Tis a Gift to Be Simple* describe this when they say, "There is a great feeling of freedom in cutting back our consumption, but often grieving is part of the process, too. Embarrassment and low self-esteem may surface when we begin to rebuild our sense of self not from our possessions or our power to buy them but from a new set of values that asks only for our 'fair share.' "[8]

When you declutter, remember to maintain balance. Don't go overboard and become extreme. Just let this statement guide you:

> Voluntary simplicity does not mean we all have to sell our homes. It doesn't even mean we can't have nice things. It may mean we can't have all of them. Like anything else, however, it does require a beginning. Moving down is like putting a pencil to our life's story and asking, "What can I cross out and still have an abundant life? What excess can I remove from my life that will help me express my true values? What parts of my life's story are distractions that only keep me off pace and running ragged?"[9]

How would you answer these three questions raised by the authors of '*Tis a Gift to Be Simple?*

- What can I cross out and still have an abundant life?

- What excess can I remove from my life that will help me express my true values?

- What parts of my life's story are distractions that only keep me off pace and running ragged?[10]

As difficult and as uncomfortable as it may be, answering these questions may be just what you need to help you simplify your life and get more out of it.

Is positive downscaling really possible? Yes, it is. You may want to try it on an experimental basis for one month and then decide whether or not this is for you. It doesn't mean that if you follow this program you will cut back by 10 percent each month! If you did, you would quickly be left with nothing. The value is to prove to yourself that downscaling and decluttering are possible to do. That's an achievement in itself!

Reducing Your Possessions

Step 1

Let's start with your filing system (for some of us, that's a joke) or where you keep any kind of papers.

- Get rid of out-of-season catalogs or any catalogs from which you know you will not order. Do the same with old phone books.

- Separate out any magazines that are over a month old. If you want to keep an article, cut it out and file it. Then toss the magazine or give it away to neighbors, the library, or maybe a convalescent home. Remember to take off your mailing label before you give it away. If you discover that you really are not reading certain magazines, cancel your subscription.

- Throw out old letters, stationery, and memos.

- Throw out contracts and service manuals for appliances you don't own anymore.

- Do you really need duplicates of everything? If it's really important, use a home safe or a safe-deposit box.

- Destroy by shredding old unneeded legal documents like records from home sales, deceased family members' tax returns or wills, and receipts that are over 15 years old. If you have questions about which receipts to save, check with a tax consultant.

- What about those dream-trip travel brochures from several years ago? Prices and itineraries change. Toss the brochures.

- Evaluate papers that are sitting on top of furniture in plain sight anywhere in your house. Ask yourself if you will really need them. When will you use them again? Decide whether to keep or toss them.

Step 2

It's time to declutter your collection of books and old magazines. The statement that usually keeps them around is, "I read these in college, and I may want to read them again." Really? How many years have you been saying this? If you have reference books that you use fairly often, keep those books. But why are these others still there? Consider donating items like:

- All old textbooks and encyclopedias.
- Foreign language books that are foreign to you now!
- Old cookbooks that you think you'll use someday. Photocopy those one or two great recipes, put them in a card file, and give away the cookbook.
- Damaged books.
- Old record albums, cassettes, eight tracks, CDs, or videos you don't use anymore.

Step 3

Keep the following items:

- Collectibles. Keep them where the dog or silverfish can't eat them.
- Old yearbooks, picture albums, scrapbooks that are "must keep" items.
- Reference materials you use.
- Items you will pass on to your children.

Step 4

Declutter closets and cupboards. Toss out or donate items like these:

- Clothes that no longer fit. If you think you're going to lose weight and wear them again, wait a month; if you haven't lost any weight after a month, get rid of those clothes.

- Clothes that you haven't worn for a year or you don't think you'll wear in the next six months.

- Any clothes your children have outgrown.

- Worn-out, damaged, or stained clothes you won't wear even as grubbies.

Step 5

Attack the house itself. Look through your house, garage, attic, and basement. Throw out or give away the following:

- Items you think you'll use someday but deep down you know you never will.

- Anything that has no value or purpose.

- Anything that is obsolete in terms of equipment or function.

- 90 percent of what you're saving in the junk drawer.

- Any food or medicine that has an old expiration date on it. If you have emergency food supplies for earthquakes, tornadoes, or snowstorms, make sure you check the expiration dates so the supplies stay usable.

- Old perishables.

Finally, remember you may need to discuss with other family members what you toss before you toss. Otherwise, you may end up with more grief than the grief caused by the clutter![11]

Keep a What-Not-to-Do List

How else can you downscale and simplify? You're aware of the value of a what-to-do list. But have you ever operated your life by a what-not-to-do list? It can be very efficient and helpful. Here's how you do it:

1. List all tasks or items that are not a priority. The least important are those items that need to wait until the important ones have been completed. You may have to fight the tendency to do what's easier, more fun, or less time consuming.

2. Don't do anything that has no value or importance for your life. If you don't do something, what's the result of not doing it? Ask the Lord to guide you to determine what to do today as well as what not to do.

3. If someone else can do a task as well as you can, let the other person do it. The desire to be in control often limits our delegating. Sure, it may take you longer the first time around to show someone else what to do and how to do it, but once the person is trained, learn to depend on that person to do that task.

4. Don't do anything merely to please people because you live in fear of their response. This isn't healthy.

5. Look back over the past six months to determine the following:
   - What you are glad you did.
   - What you wish you had done.
   - What you wish you had not done.
   - What you will change about what you will do in the future.[12]

Time for Reflection

1. Describe a time when you experienced downscaling in some way.

2. In what way would the 10 percent plan be useful in your life? Describe what you would do.

3. When will you take time to declutter your house?

4. What did you learn from completing the possessions inventory?

One Person's
Reflections on Life

- *If my life were balanced, I would feel...* as if I owned just the right number of things. My home and life would not feel cluttered.

- *To me a fulfilled life...* is more of a spiritual issue than anything else. It's putting down forever the worries, cares, and possessions of this world.

- *What keeps me from changing my life is...* fear that once I give something away, I would want it again. I want to be able to find my satisfaction in the Lord, not in my possessions.

- *If I were to have the life I always wanted, I would...* get rid of all the materialistic things that distract me from God's Word and all other unnecessary possessions that prevent me from truly living by the power of the Spirit.

- If you listed all of your canceled checks, what message would they give about the place money has in your life?

- To what extent do you operate on a well-defined budget that the entire family is aware of and has some voice in creating?

- To what extent do you have a plan to handle extra money that comes in unexpectedly? (That does happen, you know.)

- To what extent do you and your family members pray about money and the direction God wants you to take in using it for his kingdom and glory?

Your answers to these questions will be revealing and helpful.

Downscaling Spending

Our culture encourages us to think that if we want something, we need it. And if we can't afford it, we can buy it on credit or work harder and longer to get it. But before you start taking on extra jobs or working longer hours, examine the expenditure. Is it something you really need? Can you get it without buying it? Obviously, I'm not advocating stealing it, but what about borrowing the item? Can you rent it? Can you buy it used? Think creatively.

It's one thing to begin to declutter what you already have, but if you continue your pattern of accumulating, the process of a fulfilled life won't happen. Do your spending habits need alteration? How can you change? Find models of people who spend wisely. Look for people who have been able to live without debt, who give generously to charities, who save for future needs, and who seem to be free from the pressure of money. Some people provide models to us in their decisions...

- to make a commitment never to purchase any extra nonessential items without describing fully (1) how they will pay for it; (2) how it will affect their lives in both a positive and a negative way; and (3) how it will affect their family members.

- never to purchase an item on the spot, but take time to discuss it with their family members and to check three other stores to find a better price.

- to identify which items they can use credit cards for and which they cannot.

- to use only those cards that must be paid in full each month. They're aware of the fact that using credit cards increases spending by 34 percent.[3]

Other people choose to keep a firm budget, which the family sets together. Still others choose to search for alternative ways of obtaining things on which they would normally have to spend money. Some churches, for example, sponsor clothing exchanges so that people can bring their children's outgrown clothing and exchange it for clothing in the sizes they need. Some families swap babysitting responsibilities so that parents can have time away from their children without the growing expense of childcare.

The authors of *Downscaling* suggest that you

> try to let a month go by without spending money on nonessentials and see if you even notice their absence....Or you might try the 10 percent twist. Decrease the number of trinkets you buy by 10 percent. Be satisfied with 10 percent fewer clothes and accessories. Purchase 10 percent fewer groceries and waste 10 percent less in the refrigerator. Or spend 10 percent less on meals out this month. A 10 percent

change results in an almost negligible hardship, yet
the savings can add up to a substantial figure.[4]

Remember in all of this that the true source of all our money
is not our jobs and not our investments. The true source is God,
the giver of every good gift. As you think about your financial lifestyle, your money, and your spending patterns, remember that we
are merely stewards of what God chooses to give us. He promises
that if we are wise stewards, he will bless us. If we misuse what he
has given us, we will lose some of his blessing.

Time for Reflection

1. What is the greatest obstacle to your financial freedom?

2. What will you do to eliminate that obstacle?

3. How would you like to change your view of money?

4. What spending patterns need to be altered?

5. What will you do to begin the process?

6. Who are good models to you of financial balance?

One Person's
Reflections on Life

- *If my life were balanced, I would feel…* as if our lifestyle was just where it needs to be—not spending too much, not too caught up in work. Financial balance is a good goal.

- *To me a fulfilled life means…* taking walks, watching the sunrise, listening to the words "I love you, Mommy" without having to run out to go to work at the local restaurant. It's time for a kiss as my husband leaves for the day. A simple lifestyle means not having to rob from one part of my life to pay the other. That's the best way I can state it.

- *What keeps me from changing my life are…* the pressures of a mortgage, a family that needs food and clothing, medical bills that need to be paid. I would like to quit my job—who wouldn't? I'm not afraid of simplifying my life. It just feels as if we cannot afford it.

- *If I were to have the life I always wanted, I would…* find a way to leave my job, move to the country, and raise my children. I find that the bustle of daily life is very tiring. My kids and husband see me a few hours a day during the week and watch me run around doing all the chores over the weekend. If I could stay at home, I would watch my children get on the bus, walk the dog, clean my house, breathe the air, and make dinner all without complaining about how short the day seems.

10

The People Who Clutter Our Lives

At this point you may be saying, "Norm, I know how to balance my life. I'm fairly organized. I can keep things in perspective, and I'm not driven. I know what needs to be done and how to do it. I've read many books about time management, setting priorities, resting, and simplifying my life. It's not for lack of technique that I'm having difficulty simplifying my life. It's because other people complicate everything. And it's not just one person. There are several. Sometimes I feel like a juggler trying to keep everyone happy or from interfering in my plans or from trying to control my life. If they aren't creating one problem, they're creating another. Life would be great—I'd have the life I always wanted—if it weren't for people."

Despite our best efforts, often it's people who sabotage our efforts.

If you've experienced this, you're not alone. It doesn't take many years of living to discover that some individuals are more difficult to get along with than others. Those who clutter and hamper your life may be family members, coworkers, neighbors, or fellow church members. You may have tried several approaches to dealing with them. You may feel that you've exhausted yourself trying to change them or avoid what they do, only to discover that most of your efforts haven't worked. You've tried to accept them as they are, but you've only reinforced their impossible behavior and increased your feelings of being victimized, martyred, or totally frustrated. And you've tried to ignore them, but you know that's the last thing God wants you to do.

You have been frustrated because you can't find a way to relate to difficult people without driving yourself crazy or selling yourself short. And not only do these people interfere with the life you're seeking, they add to the chaos.

Difficult people come in many sizes, shapes, and forms. Some are slave drivers. Others compete with you, whether or not you want the competition. Still others seethe with anger. Let's look at two kinds of difficult people. The two mentioned in the following discussion may not be the ones who are upsetting your life, but the principles shared later in this chapter may enable you to deal with whatever type of person limits you in simplifying your life.

Negativists

Negativists can infect our lives. When you're with them, they spread gloom, despair, and discouragement. They've refined pessimism into a fine art.

I remember the story of two farmers. One was a negativist, the other an optimist.

The optimist would say, "Wonderful sunshine."

The pessimist would respond, "Yeah, I'm afraid it's going to scorch the crops."

The optimist would say, "Fine rain."

The pessimist would respond, "Yeah, I'm afraid we are going to have a flood."

One day the optimist said to the pessimist, "Have you seen my new bird dog? He's the finest money can buy."

The pessimist said, "You mean that mutt I saw penned up behind your house? He don't look like much to me."

The optimist said, "How about going hunting with me tomorrow?"

The pessimist agreed. They went. They shot some ducks. The ducks landed on the pond. The optimist ordered his dog to get the ducks. The dog obediently responded. Instead of swimming in the water after the ducks, the dog walked on top of the water, retrieved the ducks, and walked back on top of the water.

The optimist turned to the pessimist and said, "Now what do you think about that?"

Whereupon the pessimist replied, "Hmm, he can't swim, can he?"

Most people generally reflect on new ideas and approaches thoughtfully. But not negativists. They're not interested in solving problems or seeking creative alternatives. They walk around looking for a place to dump their bucket of cold water. Negativists look at most situations pessimistically, saying, "It's not worth considering. We tried it four years ago, and it didn't work then. It'll never work."

Negative people have an eroding effect on families, churches, neighborhoods, and businesses. You feel like screaming at them, "Life isn't built on defeat and despair! Why can't you be positive for a change?" But badgering them usually doesn't do any good; in fact, it may make things even worse. They'll find something wrong with any idea you share about simplifying your life. And they probably won't cooperate with your efforts to make changes you feel would help.

Negativists may not intentionally act the way they do. Some of them wish they acted differently, but they're afraid to take risks on new ideas. They struggle with disappointments. They don't want to risk failure, so they oppose any opportunity where failure is a possibility. They see themselves as lacking control over their lives, so negativism is their way of expressing control. Unfortunately, negativists' eagerness to control their own lives leads them to try to control others in the process, making them difficult to be around.

Critics

Critics are a special breed of negativist. Critics feel called to change everyone and everything around them. They seem to sit on a portable throne and pass out their negative judgments. They usually want things done their way and can be bossy as well as interfering. Boundaries don't mean much to them. If you're around critics often, don't be surprised when you feel exhausted. It's a normal response to a wearing ordeal.

If you tell critics how you're going to do something that will enhance your life, watch out. They'll find something wrong and offer advice that will complicate your situation even more. If you don't tell them and just begin a new approach, you can expect to be corrected. That's just the way they operate. Even if what you do is letter perfect, expect them to discover a flaw. They love to go through life undermining everyone else's joys and successes. They love to discount and degrade whatever you do. They could easily cultivate a feeling of defeatism and despair in your life—if you let them.

Have you ever thought of limiting the criticism you'll accept? I've decided that I won't listen to certain critics because they're not experts in the area they're criticizing. However, I will listen to the criticism of other people because I value their response. The Bible reminds us that "it is a badge of honor to accept valid criticism" (Proverbs 25:12 TLB). "A man who refuses to admit his mistakes can never be successful. But if he confesses and forsakes them, he gets another chance" (Proverbs 28:13 TLB).

As you involve yourself with negative people, avoid getting caught up in their arguments. You can't argue them out of their negativism. Their defensiveness and need for control will always push them to out-argue you, even if their arguments are illogical. You'll never win arguments with negativists.

You may think that the Christian thing to do is to follow the path of least resistance and give in to them. But giving in only feeds their problems. Jesus called us to feed his sheep, not to feed the sheep's problems. You may want to give in because you often tend to be submissive or play the victim's role, but giving in is not the loving thing to do in these cases. It only reinforces negativists' behavior.

The way you handle negativists is vital. Simply discounting their opinions and steamrolling over them will tear down your relationship. Acknowledge and affirm them by saying something like, "I now have a better understanding of your reasons for thinking the idea won't work, and I appreciate your listening to the other possibilities. But I think I'll go ahead with what I originally proposed and give it a try. However, I value your continued perspective as we move along. In the future when you have a critical comment to make, I would appreciate it if you would ask me whether or not I would like to hear it and let me make that decision. I'm sure I can count on your cooperation in this."

Negativists may or may not accept your approach. But that's not the main issue. After you've tried your best to solicit their support, you need to move on with what you know is right, regardless of their response. If you measure your success or progress by their response, you've put the control back in their hands, thus exacerbating the problem. Lovingly interact with negativists, acknowledge them, and affirm them, but be prepared to move ahead without them if they don't join you.

You can choose whether or not to let people like this determine how you think or feel about yourself and what you do. Les Parrott, author of *High-Maintenance Relationships,* tells the story of walking a friend to a newsstand, where the friend bought a paper and politely thanked the owner. But the newsstand owner didn't even acknowledge Les' friend. When Les said something about the owner's sullenness, his friend just shrugged and said, "Oh, he's that way every night." Les asked his friend why he continued to be so polite, and the man said, "Why should I let him determine how I should act?"[1]

What about you? As you travel toward simplifying your life, you'll run into negativists who will question what you do, joke about it, show disbelief in your ability to be successful, or try to make you do it their way. Will they determine what you do and how you feel? It's your choice.

Controllers

Controllers can also clutter our lives. You may live with control freaks, work with them, or be on church committees with them. They not only live their lives, but they interfere with yours as well. They can be offensive and obnoxious. The word *obnoxious* comes from a Latin word that means "to harm." And it's true. Controllers hurt relationships. In fact, studies indicate that one of the major reasons people give for "falling out of love" with their partner is that the other person has tried to control them.

Controllers push other people away. They not only complicate your life but also hinder you in trying to simplify and bring balance into your lifestyle.

I recently saw a bumper sticker that read "Born to Lead." It had a positive tone to it. I liked it. But I know some difficult people who need a similar, but not nearly as complimentary, caption attached to them: "Born to Control and Dominate." I don't believe these people were born to be so hard to get along with, but they have certainly learned to dominate and override others. I've seen them in all professions. They're hard to ignore.

Some controllers are not aware of the extent of their domineering tendencies. Others *are,* but they exercise control quietly and behind the scenes. Still others are explosive and obvious. Some of the more obnoxious controllers are very competent people, which makes them even more frustrating to be around.

It's difficult to be open and relaxed in the presence of controllers because you know what you say will be used as ammunition against you later on. And many controllers don't respond openly. They're skilled at projecting onto others the problems that exist within themselves. When you attempt to change your life, they're there to sabotage your efforts.

If you resist their dominating tendencies, controllers see it as an attack against them and their "good ideas." In response, they fall back on an extensive arsenal. Anger is a favorite mode of retaliation, expressed either loudly through shouts of irritation and sarcasm or nonverbally through "the cold shoulder" or "the silent treatment."

As you attempt to change what you do, you'll hear about it. But why should you expect any less? The controllers have been contributing to the chaos in your life all along.

One man said he feels as if he's an express train running along the fast track of life, but a controller keeps switching the tracks and sending him in several different directions. He rarely gets to his destination.

You may be controlled by an underlying threat of criticism: "Mary, just stop and think about this for a minute. You'll see that I'm right. Any intelligent adult can see this is the best way." Bingo! You're trapped. And you end up getting further away from completing your goal.

You may hear something like, "You can't really believe those books on time management! They don't know what they're talking about. Are you going to let some money-hungry promoters run your life? Come on!" These controllers are telling you that they know better than you do what's best for your life. Even in their questions there's implied criticisms and a sense of control. "You aren't really going to try to clean out those closets and toss those things away? Why would you want to do that? You'll end up wanting to use them later and regret getting rid of them."

Taking Control

What can you do with people whose behavior complicates your life? Whether the people who clutter your life are negativists, controllers, or, for that matter, competitors or martyrs, you need to take charge so that they don't run your life. How can you break loose of their influence and move ahead?

1. *Stop taking their words or actions personally.* It's true they put pressure on you. It's true they want you to live up to their standards. But they'd do this to anyone. It's *not* a personal vendetta against you. And they don't intend to hurt you. This is their lifestyle. It's a habit pattern.

2. *Don't look at them as bad or wrong.* If you do, you end up just like them. Being judgmental just activates your anger.

3. *Above all, don't accept their perception or portrayal of you.* They're trying to change you because of their own needs. If you discover an area of your life that needs change and correction, then take steps to do it for your own personal growth. Don't do it because you feel forced to by their flaw-picking suggestions. Remember, you are not the problem.[2]

4. *Don't try to fight fire with fire.* It won't work. You can't control controllers. They gain a significant amount of their power and control from those who resist them. If you decide not to pull on your end of the rope, there will be no tug-of-war. Two-thirds of the battle of resistance with controllers is in your mind. You talk with yourself about the controllers and how you feel about them. You focus on their unpleasant behavior and how you wish they would either change or leave. You probably rehearse previous encounters with them and anticipate the worst scenario at your next encounter. What happens when you keep these negative "instant replays" and "previews of coming attractions" rolling in your mind? You become physically drained, tense, and anxious. You're so focused on these

films of resistance that you are unable to concentrate on other areas in your life.

Create some new films to project in your mind, films that show you responding to the controllers in a healthy, affirming, non-intimidating manner. See yourself responding calmly instead of resisting.

5. *Find a healthy way to vent emotionally.* You need to use methods that are different from those the controllers use. Becoming a mirror image of them won't solve anything. If you express your emotion openly and intensely, expect controllers either to become defensive or to shut down completely. They won't hear you even if you're 100 percent accurate! What you say will be thrown back at you. But burying your feelings is even worse for you emotionally, physically, and spiritually. And dumping on yourself because of how you feel is no solution either.

You need a safe, healthy outlet for what's building up inside. Express your feelings aloud in prayer—with no editing. Express them to a trusted friend of the same sex, a person who can listen and reflect what you are feeling. Express your feelings through writing unmailed letters to the controllers. Keep a confidential journal of your feelings. Read your letters aloud to an empty chair or into a tape recorder. But release your feelings.[3]

6. *Determine what you will and won't tolerate.* As you learn to release your feelings, you will discover that what the controllers do or say won't affect you as much. Your new beliefs and responses will ease some of the pressure you once felt. Expect resistance to your responses. Try saying something like this to difficult people: "You may be uncomfortable with my response and resist what I am saying. I just wanted to let you know that it's all right to do that. I

expect that. You need some time to consider what I'm doing and saying. I'm not looking for an immediate response." A remark such as this takes pressure off you. It lets the other people know that you're aware of their struggle. In a sense you're now directing their response because subtly you've suggested what they could do.

At times you may have to take drastic measures with controllers. I have an answering machine at home, and sometimes I let it take all my calls. When I don't want to be bothered, I simply unplug the phone. Similarly, you may need to unplug yourself from control- lers' tactics so that you're not overwhelmed. How? You can leave the room or hang up the phone. You could say, "You have a choice. You can back up and approach me with courtesy, and we will discuss what you want or you can continue as you're doing. When you are ready to change your approach I will be willing to talk with you."

7. *Don't respond to all of their remarks and suggestions.* Ignore those that are insignificant. If they use the silent treatment, don't pursue, trying to dig out what's wrong. You might even commend them for taking some time for reflection. To help determine what you will and won't tolerate, make a list. Then reflect on it for a while.

8. *Learn to use "I" statements.* Learn how to share your feelings with controllers by using the following fill-in-the-blank sentence: "When you _____, I feel _____. What I would like is for you to _____." Here are some examples of statements like this:

- When you tell me to do each task during the day, I really feel bothered and hovered over. It also creates more work for me and wastes time. What I would like is for you to let me do things as I decide. Thank you for your cooperation.

- When you continue to check the way I'm cooking the meal, I feel like a child. I feel as if my abilities are being evaluated by someone who is not an expert, and it irritates me. What I would like is for you to let me do my job the way I do it. Then if you don't like the end result, we can discuss it to see what can be done. All right?

Notice the formula in these examples: You share your feeling, identify the unacceptable behavior, follow with a request, and then share what the other person might gain by responding to what you've said. You may also want to identify what the consequence will be if the person doesn't pay attention to your request. But make sure you are willing to follow through. For example, "If you continue to check up on me when I'm cooking, I could end up making mistakes, and I'll be less inclined to try anything new."

Establish and communicate your boundaries. The violation of a person's boundaries can occur in many relationships, but it is especially prevalent in a relationship with a controller. In a sense, you will need to teach the other person to respect you. This includes respect for what you think, how you feel, and what you do. Without this respect, you may end up like Jonah and the great fish; you may feel as if your identity has been swallowed. Setting limits and boundaries will help you change the controller's response.

When controllers blame you, confront them. Don't accept blame. That only condemns, creates guilt, and breeds resentment. You could say, "I would appreciate it if you would make your statement in a different way. I don't appreciate being blamed for this problem. Let's look at it from a different angle for a minute."[4]

Perhaps these simple suggestions will give you the hope that something different can be done. No matter what type of difficult person you're struggling with, you can take steps to bring balance to the relationship.

One of the major mistakes we make with the problem people who complicate our lives is to adjust to them rather than to learn new responses or to confront them. We learn to compensate. We allow the critics or controllers to continue, and we work harder to please them.

We may give up and begin doing just the bare minimum to exist. Why put forth the effort if others are going to mess it all up? And if we fall prey to this approach, we'll probably begin rationalizing about what we do and become negative when others talk to us about it. None of these approaches is a solution. The one thing we can do is change ourselves, our reactions, and our beliefs about the problem people and what is taking place.

Sometimes our relationships with other people are pressured because we are different from each other. Be more aware of the uniqueness of your own personality as well as the uniqueness of the other person. If your problem person is a highly structured person and if you tend to be a free-spirited person who can get lost between the front door and the car, the pressure may come from your personality differences. Neither of you is wrong; you're just different. And you need to learn to celebrate your differences.[5]

Try not to let yourself get caught in other people's problems and try not to "fix" them. You are not responsible for the way they are. Also keep your expectations of these people at a realistic level. Why expect them to be different? On the other hand, don't prejudge or blow their tendencies out of proportion. Often the people we envision in our thoughts are a far cry from who they really are. Or it could be that what we think about them becomes a self-fulfilling prophecy because of the way we end up behaving toward them.

You've probably heard the old story of the man whose car got a flat tire along a country road. When he checked the spare, he didn't have a jack. He was pretty disgusted by now. He spotted a farmhouse about a mile away, and as he headed toward the house, he said to himself, "Well, at least I can borrow a jack from that farmer, get to town, and have my tire fixed." As he walked, he heard a dog barking in the distance. He said, "I like dogs. His dog is probably a nice pooch. But it could be a vicious guard dog. And maybe the farmer is suspicious and mean. He may even come to the door with a shotgun and run me off the property." As he turned up the drive, he kept thinking in this way and got more and more upset. He walked up onto the porch, pounded on the door, and even before the friendly farmer could come to the door, the stranded motorist shouted, "You can keep your dumb jack. I didn't want it to begin with!" And he stomped off the porch.

What phantoms our minds can create!

You can learn how you tend to get hooked into whatever games the other person is playing with you. You can refuse to be a player. If you think before you respond, you can avoid ending up feeling like a victim, a rescuer, or an inept person. You can respond in a new way by tape recording an interaction and listening especially to your own side of the interaction. Then decide how you will handle the situation differently the next time.

We will always have difficult people in our lives. We can allow them to influence us in negative ways. We can allow their behavior to be our excuse for not making the necessary changes to simplify our lives. Or we can see them as catalysts for growth and allow the experience to refine us. This, like so many other things in life, is a choice.

Time for Reflection

1. What type of person complicates your life at this time?

2. How do you respond to him or her?

3. How could responding differently help you simplify your life?

4. What will you do differently in your response to this person?

One Person's
Reflections on Life

- *If my life were balanced, I would feel...* [I would] resolve my relationship with my father and reconcile relationships from my past, particularly with my former wife and her family.

- *To me a fulfilled life means...* being content with who I am and where I am.

- *What keeps me from changing my life is...* my lack of self-control. I lack the patience to deal with my father.

11

Dumping Excess
Emotional Baggage

A number of years ago my wife and I had an opportunity to take our first cruise. Since our itinerary had been selected for us in advance, our biggest task concerned selecting what we would take with us. We had never traveled by ship before, so we were unsure about what to take. As we looked at the pile of goods and clothing strewn on the living-room floor, it was hard to believe that this voyage was to last for only eight days. It looked more like a scene from *Around the World in 80 Days!* We knew that if we were not careful in selecting what we should take with us, we would end up with an incredible amount of excess baggage.

So we began to sort through the pile and ask, "Do we really need this item? Will I ever wear this outfit? What's the purpose of this gadget?

Will this item make our journey more enjoyable or will it get in the way? If I don't have this with me, will I actually have a better time?" We had to be discriminating. My wife and I eliminated much of what we had gathered.

However, even with careful selecting, we ended up taking too much. Once we arrived at the ship and the porters brought our luggage to our stateroom (That's a joke. It looked more like a closet!), we still had too many suitcases and boxes. We unpacked and hung as many clothes as we could in the closet, but it was crammed full. We went through a selection process again and put some of our belongings back in the suitcases and boxes.

Then we had the problem of storing the luggage. Stashing some of it under the bed worked fine during the day, but when we wanted to rest or sleep the bulge in the bed was uncomfortable.

We still didn't know what to do with the bags that wouldn't fit under the bed. We tried to hide them in every nook and cranny of the stateroom, but there just wasn't enough room in the cabin.

We considered tossing the excess baggage overboard. It would be out of sight and gone forever. No more problems and no more irritations! But what a price to pay. We'd feel the effects of that action for months and years to come.

We weren't successful in dealing with our extra baggage on that cruise. But we both decided that if we ever had it to do again, we would make wiser decisions. That excess baggage interfered with our comfort and enjoyment of that trip.

Excess baggage of any kind keeps us from living and experiencing a fulfilled life. Baggage comes in many shapes and sizes. It could be old behavior patterns that are counterproductive, but we've stuck with them for years. It could even be an immobilizing fear that shapes our beliefs and behaviors. Excess baggage drags us down. It makes the problems of life more difficult to handle and creates problems of its own.

Behaviors, perceptions, and emotions are excess baggage if they...

- Keep you from obtaining what you want and need in your life.

- Keep you from being comfortable with who you are as a person. If you have difficulty accepting yourself for who you are, even with your understanding of how God sees you, there's some excess baggage there.

- Keep you from being loved and accepted by others even though you deeply desire to be loved. Some people try so hard to be loved that they actually repel people.

What are some possible pieces of excess baggage you may be carrying around unnecessarily? What baggage are you carrying from your past?

Past Baggage

Some adults carry the baggage of a childhood and adolescence in which they were overly coerced. They were not taught to become responsible adults but lived with constant direction, supervision, instructions, and reminders.

Some adults carry the baggage of living with parents who were overly coerced. The parents caved to the child's demands, angry outbursts, and impulsiveness. These parents allowed the child to dictate what went on.

Some adults carry the baggage of having lived with conditional acceptance. They were asked to perform above and beyond all reasonable standards and soon developed a preoccupation with achievements.

Some adults carry the baggage of having lived with indulgent parents who lavished gifts, privileges, and services on them. They were not taught to work for anything, and they grew up expecting the world to serve them.

Some adults carry the baggage of hostility and aggression or rejection and neglect. These can be heavy burdens to carry.

You may identify with one or more of these brands of excess baggage. Learning to recognize your baggage is the first step in the process of getting rid of what is complicating your life.

Personality Baggage

We also carry around the baggage of our personality. Sometimes the excess is caused by our weaknesses and our inabilities. For example, our tendency to respond with anger or negativity may complicate our lives. Or our inability to organize ourselves or get work done may clutter our lives.

Sometimes, however, the excess baggage is rooted in our inability to balance our strengths and weaknesses. For example, you may be a structured person who has life under control. In many ways those personal qualities are positive, giving you the ability to accomplish things. But when those qualities are out of balance, they become excess baggage. Your need to be in control may express itself in an intense need to be right. You may not be able to tolerate anything short of perfection. You find yourself becoming a compulsive planner. Or you may have a personality that is just the opposite—freewheeling, spontaneous, carefree, noncommitted, adaptive.

Neither lifestyle is bad. Both are needed. We're all born with a particular bent in how we prefer to structure our lives. I've seen the evidence of this even in three-year-olds. Unfortunately, for many of us this bent intensifies and gains momentum as we grow older. It can become too much of a good thing.

Recently I watched a knee-gripping television movie about a car that was out of control. The accelerator stuck while the car was on a freeway, and the occupants couldn't do anything to stop it. The speed crept up from 60 to 90 miles per hour and stayed there. Freeways were shut down, and police were in pursuit. The car came to a halt when it ran out of gas and crashed off the freeway. People do the same thing. When their personality bent intensifies, it is out of control, too. It becomes excess baggage and hinders us from moving forward.

Heavy Pieces of Luggage

What can we do to keep ourselves from getting weighed down with excess baggage? If the first step, as we said earlier, is recognizing the presence of the baggage, the second step is examining how that baggage hinders us.

To help you examine our own heavy piece of luggage, let's take an in-depth look at one aspect of personality and at what can be done to balance the liabilities. Let's choose the overly structured person. This may not be your personality bent, but looking at it closely may help you examine your own baggage.

The overly structured person is efficient. He's thorough. The smallest detail has no chance of escaping notice. Each day—no, each hour—needs to be organized. Plans must be orderly. This kind of person schedules not only his or her own life but also yours.

The overly structured person belongs to the "list-of-the-month club." Life is run by lists because they keep it focused and in control. But lists can also be obstacles to pleasure. If a list is a guide with a minimum of emotional attachment, that's fine. But too often anything that interferes with following the list can ruin a whole day. Lists can hold some people hostage.

The overly structured person has a particular communication style—usually it's decisive, forceful, and straightforward, aimed at producing outcomes, results, and conclusions.

The overly structured person is in charge of his or her world—every aspect of it. This person is the CEO, the chairperson of the board, the treasurer, and the secretary.

Relationships, especially committed relationships, are important to the overly structured person. Comfort in relationships comes from following traditions and establishing certain ways of relating. The overly structured person may set aside a definite time each week to "work on relationships."

The words "I admit I was wrong" are like a foreign language. This person wants to be right, *needs* to be right, and will cut corners to prove it. It's like an addiction.

For this individual, neatness is a God-given virtue. Clutter and anything out of place creates stress. The overly structured person lives by three mottoes: "I ought," "I should," and "I must." These messages are played again and again. When this person isn't working or producing enough, he or she feels guilty because of all the "shoulds."

I have seen this kind of control in the mother who complained about how much she had to do and how no one appreciated her efforts as she *selected* and laid out her three teenage daughters' clothes each evening for the next day. I've seen it in the father who complained that his family avoided him. Could he feel that way because he told the children what and how much they could eat at dinner each night? If they ate too much, he reached over and took the food right out of their mouths. I've seen it in the parent who makes a sweep through the house three times per day to pick up anything out of place and then gripes about having to pick up after everyone else.

I've known clients who "must have" their socks folded, lined up by color, and placed an inch apart in their drawer. When it's not that way, their spouse is berated (which, incidentally, is emotional abuse). I've been with those whose structured approach makes them hover over their partners with a timer and a critical tirade just waiting to be unleashed when they find a mistake.

Is this the way we were called to live? No! Is this the way God wants anyone to live? No! It's a cluttered, unhealthy way of living.

Risk for a Change

What can be done? Or can anything be done? If you have seen yourself in the preceding paragraphs or if you have seen those same dynamics in some other personality bent that is out of control in your life, take heart. You *can* change. But change involves risk. You will have to face the fact that...

- you'll be giving up some of your identity.
- someone else may know a better way.
- simplifying your life involves an inner lifestyle change.
- you will feel as if you are losing control.

But the result is a balanced, relaxed, satisfying, more productive life. I know. I've seen it in those who take the risk to create balance.

So what do you do now? Take that first step. Risk it.

Howard Hughes, one of the richest men of the twentieth century, was a good example of what can happen when we risk—and when we refuse to take risks. Hughes had a great impact on the aircraft industry, helping the United States maintain dominance in the sky during several wars. He helped establish the movie industry and influenced the entertainment industry. He gained tremendous power, and his power affected not only our country and society but the world.

Howard Hughes was a consummate risk taker for a large part of his life. But then he changed. He redirected his energies and became a fanatic, protecting himself against risk. He created a virtual prison for himself in his attempt to insulate himself from decisions, people, germs, or anything else he perceived to be a risk. He had accumulated billions, but he chose to live in a hotel room and vegetate until he died. He ended up a fearful old man who didn't trust anyone. He was a prisoner when he could have been free. When Howard Hughes stopped risking, he stopped living.[1]

Do you feel the need to make some changes in your lifestyle? Let's consider some questions about this proposed change.

1. What are the risks involved? You may be uncomfortable with the outcome. You may not feel as secure. You may wonder how others will respond. These are all legitimate. However, the results may be just the opposite. You may find yourself comfortable with the outcome. You may feel very secure. And people may respond positively toward your change. Have you ever considered those possibilities? It may be worth the risk.

2. What are the advantages of changing? You may discover a more relaxed, fulfilling lifestyle that others will appreciate as well.

3. Does the change involve a risk to anyone else? The only risk is how others will handle the positive change they see in your life. You may find them becoming cheerleaders.

4. How can you reduce the risk? Just becoming aware of the effort involved in making the change and how others may react at first will reduce your perceived risk.

How do you begin? You start small and learn to do the opposite of what you usually do. I'm going to give several suggestions, and your initial response will probably be "Yes, but" or "You have no idea what could happen if I do that." That's all right. State your objections. List them. Read them aloud. Then deny them. Discard them. They're controlling you, making you their victim, and keeping you from changing. Here are some suggestions for doing the opposite of what you usually do:

1. If you usually drive, let someone else do it.

2. If you usually handle the checkbook, let someone else do it.

3. If you usually determine what's for dinner, let someone else do it.

4. If you usually choose the restaurant, TV program, or movie, let someone else do it.

5. If you usually choose what others wear, let someone else do it.

6. If you usually plan where to go on vacation, let someone else do it.

If you take these risks and allow someone else to make the decisions, *don't* correct, guide, or criticize the other person. Relax and go along with it. You're going to get something out of this. Just think, you've saved time. You didn't have to plan. You've discovered you can live without always being in control. But the best part is how you shock people. I love this. I'm fairly predictable. When I'm not predictable, it throws people off. Whenever I'm casual about being on time, it shocks them. When I say I'm going to play something by ear instead of having it planned, it surprises them. I'm still planning; I'm just planning to be unplanned!

Once you've accomplished this change, it's time to tackle the messages that control your life: the "oughts," "shoulds," and "musts."

Dr. Judith Sills suggests a number of ways you can begin to change your overly structured pattern of living. Some of these you may laugh at. Others may cause you to cringe at even thinking of doing them. But why not? Be adventuresome. Prove to yourself that you can grow and change. Now, if these suggestions reflect the way you typically do things, you may need to go the opposite way and structure your life more.

1. Put your clothes away in places they don't usually go. Put your socks in a sweater drawer, or hang up shirts/blouses with skirts or slacks.

2. Balance half of your checkbook on one day, and do the other half a few days later.

3. Pay your bills a week later than you usually do.

4. Leave the dishes on the table for an hour after dinner. Then don't wash them until the next day.

5. Instead of eating three main meals a day, eat several snacks.

6. Don't hang up your clothes right away when you take them off.

7. Don't make your bed for three days.

8. Don't wash the car, mow the lawn, or do laundry on the day or at the time you usually do.

9. Don't open your mail for two days.

10. If you watch TV, don't. If you don't, do!

11. Don't answer your phone messages or e-mail until the end of the day.

Right now you're thinking, *This is dumb. This isn't going to help my life. It's going to clutter it up even more.* That's impossible. The purpose of this is to help you experience *change.* To help you discover your potential for being different so you can learn to live a less cluttered life.[2]

Time for Reflection

1. What excess baggage are you carrying around from your past? How can you lighten the load?

2. What personality bent is a piece of excess baggage for you?

3. What strengths have turned into excess baggage for you? List two or three steps you can take to bring your strengths back into balance.

4. If you were to describe your personality with several descriptive terms, what would they be? In what way do these personality bents help either to balance your life or clutter it?

5. Which of the suggestions at the conclusion of the chapter will you implement?

One Person's
Reflections on Life

- *If my life were balanced, I would feel*…more balanced, less anxious, more content with myself and my surroundings.

- *To me a fulfilled life means*…little or no strife in the family, not a lot of anxiety.

- *What keeps me from changing my life is*…emotional baggage, both from my past and from relationships.

12

Doing the Best Thing

Sacred cows. The term originated in the cultures in which cows were considered sacred. They were protected. You couldn't eat them. They had rights. And they were untouchable. I think I've discovered another sacred cow. I stumbled on it while looking for information and resources for this chapter on how to simplify your spiritual life. I was amazed that few people had ever addressed this issue. It's as if we're treading on hallowed ground.

No one wants to address the issue of a cluttered, overinvolved spiritual life. In fact, many people would argue that the phrase "over-involved spiritual life" is an impossibility. How could people be *over-involved* spiritually? Isn't the problem that most Christians aren't involved enough, committed enough, or busy enough in their church or fellowship?

Over the years I've heard comments like these: "We need to become weary in well doing" or "You need to burn yourself out for Jesus." It's true a lot of people in the church are "casual drop-ins." It's been said that in the local church, 10 percent of the people do 90 percent of the work. If this is so, it's unfortunate because it means many people are serving in areas in which they're not gifted. And they will become overloaded and burn out—eventually they may even drop out. Or they will become so entrenched in the church that they end up believing it belongs to them, and they will start controlling it. Listen to what two people said about their involvement in church:

> I used to be involved in church. I wasn't just involved; I was in it up to my head. At one time I was serving on four committees, teaching, and leading a men's group. I thought I was really living the Christian life. The problem was that I felt no contentment. I was busy but not satisfied. I was doing but had no relationship with the Lord. I'd sit in the worship service, but I didn't worship. Oh sure, people praised me and said they couldn't do it without me. The sad thing was I believed them. I kept on and on. I got more and more weary. Part of it was I'm no teacher. I hate teaching. It's not my gift. I dreaded preparing. And all this stuff kept me from my family. One day I had no more to give. So I quit. I quit it all. Slowly I'm building a relationship with the Lord. That's got to be there; that has to come first.

> I don't know when I've attended a worship service. I'd like to, but it seems that they always need me in the nursery. I wish they'd get others, but it's hard to find committed people. I tried to quit, but I felt so guilty when I heard the pastor's concerns about nursery coverage that I stayed on. I guess I can do without the worship and just serve.

What's your level of involvement in your church? Is it balanced? What's your level of involvement in the Christian life? Is it balanced? Are you serving Christ in some way? If so, who called you to this service?

Just as we asked this question earlier about other areas of our life, we need to ask it again spiritually: "Why are you doing what you are doing?" Too many people who work for the Lord end up exhausted. Too many people end up with no spiritual strength to draw on because their spiritual reservoir is empty. We all want the abundant Christian life. But the abundance often describes our activity, not our spiritual growth.

Taking Stock of Your Spiritual Life

The pattern of overinvolvement, clutter, and busyness that's a part of our lives at home and at work *will* follow us into our spiritual lives unless we are vigilant. People often look to their church and spiritual lives as a little oasis of refreshment—a place where they meet the living God who will help them make sense out of the chaos in their lives. Sadly, the "oasis" is frequently just another place of breathlessness and stress. Does your spiritual life refresh you or exhaust you?

- How is your life—your attitude and your behavior—different after you've concluded your time of devotions?

- How is your life—your attitude and your behavior—different after you've come from a worship service?

- How is your life—your attitude and your behavior—different after you've finished teaching that class or walked out of that board meeting?

You've seen families (perhaps yours?) who speed into the church parking lot late, pull to a stop, fling the doors open before the car stops, spill out, and begin running in different directions. It's Sunday morning! (Or Wednesday or Thursday or Friday evening.) They rush home the same way and continue their busyness. There's nothing relaxed or worshipful about this experience.

As the programs and services proliferate within the church, the demands on members' time increase. In his book *Restoring Your Spiritual Passion,* pastor and author Gordon MacDonald describes the conflict well. "More time for activity means less time for devotions. Doing more *for* God may mean less time *with* God. Talking becomes an effective substitute for meditating or listening. After all, something says to us, doing all these noble things isn't all bad. No, it may be good; but it may not always be best."[1]

What does it mean to do the best thing? Jesus addresses that question in his interactions with his friends Martha and Mary. You know the story. When he visited with the women, one chose to serve him by preparing a meal, and the other chose to stop her activity and listen to what he had to say. When the busy woman complained that the other wasn't helping her, Jesus said, "Only one thing is needed. Mary has chosen what is better" (Luke 10:2 NIV). Often we are like the busy sister. We assume serving actively is the most effective way to show our love for the Lord. And sometimes it is. But we need to be open to what the Lord says is the best thing for us to do. Sometimes that may be sitting quietly, listening to what he has to say to us.

We face serious consequences when we overdo in any area of life. Eventually we come to the place where we're drained. I know. I experience this for two days after conducting a seminar. I've seen this occur in the men and women who serve at their church day after day with no letup. At first they have deep inner resources on which to draw. In time, though, depletion sets in, and their spirits become exhausted. When we're overworked and drained spiritually, we end up with self-doubts and increasing negativity. Criticism sets in, and it's directed not only toward others but also at ourselves. Gordon MacDonald says, "You can't do work of a spiritual nature without energy going out of you."[2] Jesus felt it acutely when a sick woman reached out and touched the bottom of his robe. He said, "Someone...touched me, for I felt healing power go out from me" (Luke 8:46).

History of Your Spiritual Life

One way to assess where you need balance is to do a history of your spiritual life and your church involvement over the past ten years. Using the "Spiritual History" chart, list the activities you've been involved in, and rate your personal walk with the Lord for each year. Include in your list of activities not only your involvement at church and in your community but also your personal disciplines such as personal Bible study, personal retreats, and seminars.

Before filling in your own history, take a look at Jim's chart. Filling in his chart helped him understand what he needs to do in the future.

FINDING THE LIFE YOU'VE BEEN LOOKING FOR

Jim's Spiritual History		
Years	Number of Activities	Walk with the Lord 1=close; 5=distant
10 years ago	6	4
9 years ago	6	2
8 years ago	4	3
7 years ago	3	3
6 years ago	1	4
5 years ago	2	5
4 years ago	1	5
3 years ago	4	4
2 years ago	5	2
1 year ago	4	3
This year	4	4

Now, fill in this chart to represent your personal history. If you need help remembering what responsibilities and activities you were involved in several years ago, fill in the "Activity Chart" also. It may jog your memory.

_____ Spiritual History		
Years	Number of Activities	Walk with the Lord 1=close; 5=distant
10 years ago		
9 years ago		
8 years ago		
7 years ago		
6 years ago		
5 years ago		
4 years ago		
3 years ago		
2 years ago		
1 year ago		
This year		

Activity Chart						
Years	Activity	Activity	Activity	Activity	Activity	Activity
10 years ago						
9 years ago						
8 years ago						
7 years ago						
6 years ago						
5 years ago						
4 years ago						
3 years ago						
2 years ago						
1 year ago						
This year						

What does this assessment tell you about your spiritual life? Is it in balance? Maybe you have discovered that your spiritual life is in balance; you have set aside appropriate times for personal time with God, and you are energized by involvements. Or maybe you have discovered that you are *doing* a lot but are not growing or deepening as a result of your study or service or teaching or involvement in a group. If you are in the latter category, you may want to back off from what you are doing and reassess your spiritual life.

You may want to take your own personal retreat. One man took a half-day to reflect on his spiritual life. He spent it in the sanctuary of his church when no one was around or would bother him. He prayed, read Scripture aloud, sang hymns, and sat in various pews in the church. He studied the stained-glass windows, which he noticed in detail for the first time. His prayer was simple, "Lord, draw me closer to you. Show me what you want and don't want me to do."

As you look at what you are involved in at the present time, ask the Lord to show you what's important to him. Ask him to show you where you need to spend more time or less time. Ask him what you need to add or to drop in your life.

In his book *The Source of My Strength,* Charles Stanley lists some questions that may help you assess your activity level.

- Ask about each activity: "Lord, is this something you really want me to do, and something you want me to do right now? Do you really want me to spend this much time at it? Do you want me to spend more time?"

- Don't be bound to your list. Also ask the Lord: "Is there something else you'd rather I spend my time doing? Is there something I'm not doing that you would like for me to do?"

- Ask yourself: "What are the consequences of taking a new position? What are the consequences of taking the action I propose to take?"[3]

If you genuinely feel called to serve in some Christian endeavor, God will provide the means for you to have the energy and resources to accomplish the task. Remember that God does not commit himself to helping us do everything *we* want to do in our lives, but to helping us do the things *he* wants us to do.[4]

If you feel your life is cluttered and if you're overwhelmed with the spiritual activity in your life, keep in mind what Malcolm Smith says:

> A person is healed of burnout when he receives a fresh revelation of who God is….We would be satisfied if there was a demonstration of power that ordered life in the way we feel it would show God's glory the best.
>
> We come to God and demand a formula, a series of steps we can tell others we followed to get out of the pit of spiritual exhaustion. But God frustrates us. He doesn't give us a formula….He gives us Himself. Understand who He is, and everything begins to fall into place. The answer to spiritual burnout is to respond to God afresh and discover a new relationship with Him.
>
> The "sound of a gentle blowing" has become flesh and lived among us in Jesus. The gospel is that He has risen out of death, is now alive and by His Spirit, is breathing His life into our weary, tattered spirits and making us whole.[5]

Finding Balance in Worship

At the heart of our spiritual experience is our personal relationship with God. Our relationship is not based on activities or even service. It is founded on worship and time spent with God. Where and when do you worship? You may attend a "worship service," but do you worship? Are you in a place where you focus on God—on his greatness, his character?

How do you define worship? Is it a solemn experience? Is it restrictive? Is it one hour on Sunday? Is it a duty? It's really none of these. Worship comes out of the Old English word *wearth-scipe*. It means that someone ascribed "worth" to the object of their "wearthscipe," or worship. When you worship, you are ascribing great worth to God. In Revelation we see glimpses of true worship. John describes a choir of millions of angels shouting with loud voices: "Worthy is the Lamb, who was slain, to receive power and wealth and wisdom and strength and honor and glory and praise!" (Revelation 5:12 NIV).

In his book *Seeking God Together,* David Stoop describes the process of worship:

> Richard Foster, in *Celebration of Discipline,* writes that worship "involves our whole being. The body, mind, spirit, and emotions should all be laid on the altar of worship. Often we forget that worship would include the body as well as the mind and the spirit." We worship with our whole being when we sing together, but are there other ways we, as a couple, bring our bodies into our worship?
>
> Habakkuk tells us that "the Lord is in his holy Temple; let all the earth be silent before him" (Habakkuk 2:20). Have you ever sat in silence and watched a sunset? Then you know of one way to worship God in silence. Perhaps you've sat in some crowded place together in silence. Remember the first truth in our process of developing spiritual intimacy—that God is already at work around us. Why not look for God's activity? What might God be up to? After the silence, talk about your impressions. Notice the distractions. Do they have any special meaning to you? Learn to listen to the inner voice of the Holy Spirit as you sit in silence.
>
> We had an interesting experience in worship recently. Our pastor asked us to think of something we would like to thank God for—something current in our life, whether small or large. Then he explained that after singing the next

song, we were all to applaud and our applause would be directed to God. He talked about how we applaud great plays in sports, great performances in theater, and inspiring, courageous actions by other people. "Applause," he added, "is to give praise to someone worthy of praise."

After we sang the chorus, the whole congregation applauded God, something we hadn't done as a congregation before. We had applauded God for general things before, but not for some particular involvement he had had in our lives. Here are the words to the chorus we sang:

> We applaud Your greatness,
> We applaud Your might,
> And we shout to God in triumph
> As we set ourselves to fight;
> Ev'ry demon trembles
> When they hear our voices raised,
> Joined with loud applause affirming
> You are worthy to be praised.[6]

Worship can occur spontaneously. Some of us make it formal and structured, for that fits our personality. Yet if we would purposely entertain the possibility of spontaneous worship, we may be surprised by God. Worship is also a discipline that is uncomfortable for some people. But discipline may not be what you think it is.

When we describe worship as a discipline, we are talking about what Brother Lawrence, a seventeenth-century monk, described; we are "practicing the presence of God" in our lives on a regular basis. Brother Lawrence wrote, "I cannot imagine how religious persons can live satisfied without the practice of the presence of God."

Brother Lawrence was a humble monk whose life was very routine and boring. He worked in the monastery kitchen most of his life. If one were to look at the externals of his life, he would hardly attract any attention. But as he went about the mundane events of his daily existence, he developed the discipline of constantly being aware that God was present with him. As he peeled potatoes, he practiced an awareness of God's presence. As he swept the kitchen floor, God was there with him. When he went to worship, it was easy for him to know that God was there also, for he had experienced God's presence with him in the kitchen.

It also worked wonders with his own attitude toward his kitchen duties. If my inner focus is on God's presence with me as I scrub the pots and pans, who notices the grimy dishwater? Brother Lawrence added, "The time of business does not with me differ from the time of prayer; and in the noise and clatter of my kitchen, while several persons are calling for different things, I possess God in as great tranquility as if I were on my knees...." This kind of attitude doesn't just happen; it's a way of thinking only arrived at through discipline.

There is also a sense of freedom we experience as a result of the discipline of worship. The soul of the worshiper knows the truth of the chorus, "Set my spirit free, that I may worship thee." There is also a spirit of humility as well as a contentment that comes from this kind of worship. And, as Brother Lawrence demonstrates, out of this freedom within our worship comes our ability for genuine service.[7]

Comprehending Who God Is

Perhaps the major question in all of this is, "Why are you doing what you're doing spiritually?" What is the basis of your faith and your response to who God is and what he has done for you? Is your faith centered on God—the God of the Scriptures? Too often we miss discovering who God really is because we have created him in the image of who we want him to be. This is why I read *The Knowledge of the Holy* by A.W. Tozer and *Knowing God* by J.I. Packer each year. These books are based on scriptural understanding of the attributes of God. I need these reminders. Have you ever read these or any resource that accurately portrays the God of your faith? I've always liked what J.I. Packer says about our relationship with God:

> What matters supremely, therefore is not, in the last analysis, the fact that I know God, but the larger fact which underlies it; the fact that *He knows me.* I am graven on the palms of His hands. I am never out of His mind. All my knowledge of Him depends on His sustained initiative in knowing me.
>
> There is tremendous relief in knowing that His love to me is utterly realistic, based at every point on prior knowledge of the worst about me, so that no discovery now can disillusion Him about me, in the way I am so often disillusioned about myself, and quench His determination to bless me.[8]

Our understanding of who God is and how he wants to bless our lives is enriched when we realize that he is committed to performing good in our lives. Consider what God's Word says about his love for us:

> Surely your goodness and unfailing love will pursue me all the days of my life, and I will live in the house of the LORD forever (Psalm 23:6).
>
> And I will make an everlasting covenant with them, promising not to stop doing good for them. I will put a desire in their hearts to worship me, and they will never

leave me. I will rejoice in doing good to them and will faithfully and wholeheartedly replant them in this land (Jeremiah 32:40-41).

A few years ago, the choir at church sang an anthem based on Zephaniah 3:17. I had never heard the song before. The words were printed in our church bulletin, and I have read them many times since because they encourage me, inspire me, and remind me of what I mean to God:

> And the Father will dance over you in joy!
> He will take delight in whom He loves.
> Is that a choir I hear singing the praises of God?
> No, the Lord God Himself is exulting over you in song!
> And He will joy over you in song!
> My soul will make its boast in God,
> For He has answered all my cries.
> His faithfulness to me is as sure as the dawn of a new day.
> Awake my soul, and sing!
> Let my spirit rejoice in God!
> Sing, O daughter of Zion, with all of your heart!
> Cast away fear for you have been restored!
> Put on the garment of praise as on a festival day.
> Join with the Father in glorious, jubilant song.
> God rejoices over you in song![9]

In his fascinating book *The Pleasures of God,* John Piper beautifully expresses how God desires to do good to all who hope in him. Piper talks about God singing and asks, "What would it be like if God sang?" What do you hear when you imagine the voice of God singing?

> I hear the booming of Niagara Falls mingled

with the trickle of a mossy mountain stream. I hear the blast of Mount St. Helens mingled with a kitten's purr. I hear the power of an East Coast hurricane and the beauty of the barely audible puff of a night snow in the woods. And I hear the unimaginable roar of the sun, 865,000 miles thick, 1,300,000 times bigger than the earth, and nothing but fire, 1,000,000 degrees centigrade on the cooler surface of the corona. But I hear this unimaginable roar mingled with the tender, warm crackling of logs in the living room on a cozy winter's night.

I stand dumbfounded, staggered, speechless that God is singing over me—one who has dishonored him so many times and in so many ways. It is almost too good to be true. He is rejoicing over my good with all his heart and soul. He virtually breaks forth into song when he hits upon a new way to do me good.[10]

Have you caught the significance of how God feels about you and what he wants for you? Is your faith growing or is just your involvement or activity level growing? Perhaps the chart you completed earlier in this chapter will help you determine your growth pattern.

Worship Through Service

Do you feel free to serve the Lord and others? The freedom we have in Christ moves us to serve. It's not done out of conformity or guilt or works. Galatians 5:13 says, "For you have been called to live in freedom—not freedom to satisfy your sinful nature, but freedom to serve one another in love." *This is why we are to do what we do!*

Dave Stoop suggests that the discipline of service enhances our ability to follow Jesus more closely:

> Acts of service done out of a spirit of love and compassion may or may not do anything in terms of my own spirituality. They can simply be caring acts. But when service is a discipline, then my own spiritual life will be challenged by what I do.
>
> Second, it is a service I would not be able to do apart from the Holy Spirit's work in my life. For example, Jesus says we are to love our enemies. Love is not my natural response. And sometimes loving my enemies means that I serve them in some way. That spirit of serving will be there only through the grace of God.
>
> Third, we are exercising the discipline of service when we have a servant mind-set, which involves both motivation and a conscious decision to serve.[11]

Richard Foster suggests that true service occurs because of the enabling of the Holy Spirit rather than our own efforts. No act of service is too small. Rather than gain the favor and attention of others, we are content with what we are doing even if no one else knows about it. We're not picky about whom we serve; we're willing to serve anyone. We're not tied to results but rather want our relationship with God to grow. And when we serve, we do so out of choice.[12]

If your faith is growing, every area of your life will improve, especially the areas of relationships and balance. If our faith doesn't prompt us to love more, something is out of balance.[13]

What does it means to "do the best thing" in your life? I hope that this chapter has given you the insights, resolve, and courage to reach for the best thing. For you, that may mean saying no to some activities you have done for years. They may be good things, but they may not be the best things. Or, for you, the best thing may be saying yes to some things about which you have been hesitant to make a commitment. I hope that whatever it is, you find spiritual balance that will enable you to have the life you've always wanted.

Time for Reflection

1. What do you and others say is your area of giftedness in serving Christ?

2. Describe a time when you experienced joy and contentment in your involvement in the church.

3. What would give your spiritual life better balance? What do you need to drop? What do you need to add?

4. What would you like your relationship with Christ to be like? What can you do to begin that process?

One Person's
Reflections on Life

🌱 *If my life were balanced, I would feel…*spiritually balanced. My priorities would be based on God's will for my life, and my choices would flow from those priorities.

🌱 *To me a fulfilled life means…*having continual communication with God at the same time that I live in the real world of work, family, and responsibilities. If God is at the center, at the control panel of my life, then the rest will happen as it should.

🌱 *What keeps me from changing my life is…*my blindness to who God is. I incorrectly believe that it's all up to me, that if I don't do the right things at the right time, my life will fall apart. I need to trust wholly and completely on God and his willingness and ability to direct me.

🌱 *If I were to have the life I really wanted, I would…*find more effective ways to focus on God's character. I would allow that reality to speak above the clatter of the voices of our culture.

13

Letting Our Souls
Catch Up to Our Bodies

"Rest? You've got to be kidding. Even if I ever find time for rest, I can't rest. When I sit or lie down, I don't really rest. I feel wired. My mind keeps going. My body could be horizontal, but my mind is vertical and racing. I'd like some rest. I'd like to wake up some morning rested. But I just don't know how."

For some people, *rest* is a four-letter word meaning "unnecessary, wasteful, lazy." These people see rest as a vice and work as a virtue. "If I rest, I'll miss out on the life I've always wanted."

We're somewhat confused when it comes to activities other than work. As Gordon Dahl says, "Most middle-class Americans tend to worship their work, to work at their play, and to play at their worship. As a result, their meaning and values are distorted. Their relationships disintegrate faster than they can keep them in repair, and their lifestyles resemble a cast of characters in search of a plot."[1]

If you have pets, especially cats, you know that they like to rest a lot. And when cats want to sleep, you can do very little to get them to play. It's as if they carry around a "Do Not Disturb" sign most of the day. Rest for them is a top priority, while for many of us rest is the last priority. We steal from times of rest and recuperation to pay for work and pleasure.

We're a society that's become weary for lack of rest. We're people who reflect the psalmist's words, "I am weary with my sighing" (Psalm 6:6 NASB). The word *weary* can mean "faint, having nothing more to give, ready to collapse." Do these words describe you? Are you ready to collapse emotionally, physically, or spiritually? Are you weary? Take some time to reflect on the following questions. Be honest with yourself.

- Do you feel that there are not enough hours in the day for you to accomplish all that you or others want you to do?

- Do other people turn you into a juggler by giving you too many things to keep in the air at one time?

- Do you feel you've got to hurry, hurry, hurry to get it all done but then end up feeling as if you didn't accomplish that much?

- Do you agree to take on lots of responsibilities but end up feeling guilty when you can't complete them?

- Do you become impatient and irritable for no apparent reason?

- Do you struggle to relax because of the pressure of tasks that are not completed?

- Are you losing your ability to concentrate?

- Are you repeating yourself, forgetting names, or day-dreaming?

- Are you so overloaded or tired that your personal time with the Lord and his Word is suffering?

- Is your attendance at church either infrequent or a sterile duty that has no impact on your life?

- Are you struggling more with temptation and finding yourself reflecting a weak Christian lifestyle because your connection with God is weak?[2]

Your answers to these questions will give you some insight into your need for rest.

Leisure

We live in a leisure-oriented society. *Leisure* is a popular word in our vocabulary, but we don't really know what it means. Definitions include freedom from work, opportunity to rest, unhurried quiet, relaxation, stillness, peace, and reprieve. Did you notice, as I did, that some words are missing in that list? Look again. The word *play* isn't there. But we often equate play and leisure. I don't see the word *game* either. We often equate games with leisure. And nowhere in the list is the word *recreation*. Leisure is not synonymous with activity.

Unfortunately, leisure, like everything else, has become victim to the schedule. It's become a rushed obligation, and too often it's performed in tandem with something else.

Often what we do in our leisure time reflects how we handle work. Our leisure becomes just another expression of competition, a way of standing out from the crowd.[3]

Let's go a bit further to see what we've done with this word. *Leisure* comes from the Latin word *licere,* which means "to be permitted." Some people give themselves permission to experience leisure. Others don't. What do you give yourself permission to do or not do? The Latin word for work is *negotium,* which could be translated "non-leisure." It seems that work was secondarily defined as it related to leisure. That's not what our society does. We look at leisure as "nonwork."[4] Tim Hansel says,

> Someone once defined leisure as "an attitude of mind and a condition of the soul that fosters a capacity to perceive the reality of the world." Jesus said, "I am the light of the world. The man who follows me will never walk in the dark, but will live his life in the light" (John 8:12). Leisure can, if we permit it, become an intersection of the timeless qualities of life. Prayer, *recreation mentis in Deum* ("the recreation of the soul in God"), is necessarily an act of leisure. Play, when our spirits finally respond to Jesus' command to be more childlike, is an expression of not only the value of leisure, but of life itself. And love, if it ever becomes "work," will become imprisoned and powerless, and the greatest shaping force on earth will be lost.
>
> Leisure is more than just nonwork. It is a point of contact with reality and a catalyst for new experiences, new ideas, new people, and new places. It is the time when the gift of wholeness again becomes a hope and a possibility.[5]

If you believe what you read in the ads about leisure, you end up believing that in order to *experience* leisure, you've got to buy something and go somewhere. If this is true, then we will never experience leisure—or rest, which is even more necessary.

Even though we see *rest* and *leisure* as synonymous, they are not. In fact, for many people leisure is not at all restful. Leisure and vacations are just different directions in which to exert energy. People return home from their vacations saying, "I need a vacation now to rest up from my vacation!" We're so used to activity that leisure is just another expression of it. Many people work hard, play hard, and experience rejuvenating rest only rarely.[6]

We all have to work at rest. In his book *The Freedom of Simplicity,* Richard Foster describes his battle for rest:

> After a certain amount of immersion in public life, I begin to burn out. And I have noticed that I burn out inwardly long before I do outwardly. Hence, I must be careful not to become a fanatic bundle of hollow energy, busy among people but devoid of life. I must learn when to retreat, like Jesus, and experience the recreating power of God….And along our journey we need to discover numerous "tarrying places" where we can receive "heavenly manna."[7]

It may shock you to realize that the Bible has a lot to say about rest. Rest was God's idea. When he finished the work of creation, Genesis tells us, "for in six days the LORD made heaven and earth, but he rested on the seventh day and was refreshed" (Exodus 31:17). As some have suggested, the phrase can be translated "He refreshed himself." It's not that God needed rest; rather, he was showing us the rhythm *we* need.

Finding Balance and Rhythm

We've been taught and pushed to produce. Those who produce the most, regardless of the cost, are held up as the ideal. The problem is, they're out of sync and out of balance. We need healthy models of people who know how to rest. When you listen to a quality band or orchestra, all the parts work together in harmony. The music has balance and rhythm. Without rhythm, the music is awkward and out of sync. It just doesn't flow right.

Have you ever felt as if your life isn't flowing right, as if you've lost the rhythm? To have balance and rhythm in your life, four ingredients are necessary: rest, worship, play, and work. Too many of us change and reverse these ingredients and end up with work, work, work, and perhaps a little play.[8]

During Jesus' years on earth, he worked at maintaining balance and rhythm in his activity and rest. Dr. David McKenna, former president of Asbury Seminary, comments on how Jesus maintained the balance:

> Jesus withdraws to the sea with His disciples in order to regain His balance in the rhythm of life. During His ministry in Galilee, the rhythm has been reduced to constant work with little rest. In fact, when He goes to the synagogues for worship, He meets either human need that requires work or spiritual hardness that requires contest. Worship and work may have become so intermingled that Jesus senses the potential loss of the effective edge in His work and the fine-tuning of His communion with God. In modern terms, He might have been on the borderline of "executive burn-out."...His withdrawal to the sea is not cowardice (or laziness), it is a credit to His intuitive sense that the time has come for rest and play.[9]

Rest for Our Emotions

We need rest for our physical bodies, but even more for our emotions and our spirits. In his book *The Rhythm of Life*, Richard Exley shares these insights:

> Most of our work is not physically demanding, and yet we often drag home hardly able to put one foot in front of the other. Compare our exhaustion with the satisfied tiredness our grandparents felt at the end of their day. They were tired too, but it was from the outside-in. Ours, I think, is just the opposite. We're tired from the inside-out. Our weariness is more emotional than physical. Our spirits are depleted. The constant pressure, the continual interactions with people, taxes our emotional energies. Add a touch of interpersonal conflict, and the drain increases dramatically.
>
> A good night's sleep helps, but it cannot restore our spiritual and emotional energies unless it is supplemented by the inner disciplines of renewal—silence, solitude, and inwardness.[10]

We can have an emotional overload because of the busyness and stress of our lives. We overtax our emotions. Worry, anger, and depression are our companions. *Quiet* and *solitude* seem like words from another generation. It's work to find anything that resembles quiet. The noise level of restaurants has made a "quiet dinner out" a rare experience. Even there our nerves end up being jarred. When our emotions become overloaded, our experiences can turn into burdens and wounds. When our emotional life is weary, it becomes a catchall for emotional baggage. This keeps us from being all we want to be—all God wants us to be.

Fear

Two of the emotions that seem to rage out of control when we're weary are fear and its companion, worry. Our busyness and clutter can feed our fears and worries. We were not created to live in fear, yet some of us do. We were not designed to be motivated or driven by fear, yet some of us are.

Occasionally people tell me they are afraid of death. That's quite common. But even more people I talk to are afraid of life. Living life to its full potential is a threat to them. They are emotionally paralyzed and refuse to participate in many of life's normal experiences. They are immobilized by fear.

There is a difference between being afraid and being immobilized by fear. Physical paralysis is a terrible thing. To be locked up, immobilized so that your body cannot function and cannot respond to the messages of your mind, is very frustrating. But it is even more frustrating when the paralysis is a limitation not of the body but of the mind.

How strange it is for Christians to choose to imprison themselves in fear, especially when Christ came to set captives free! We have freedom in Christ, yet we often choose to walk through life in a bubble of fear, shut away from people and experiences. The fear of life is actually more debilitating than the fear of death. Fear disables. Fear shortens life. Fear cripples our relationships with others. Fear blocks our relationship with God. Fear makes life a chore.

In Charles Stanley's book *The Source of My Strength*, he suggests what we can do to counter our fear:

> As you begin to read the Word of God and absorb it into your life, the Spirit of God moves to drive out your fears. The process is a fairly straightforward one: The more you focus on who God is and what God is like, the more your attitude and your thinking will begin to change. You will begin to line them up with the truth of God's Word. You will begin to feel and think the way God feels and thinks.

As you begin to feel and think like God feels and thinks, fears fall away. A sense of confidence and assurance builds. You will find yourself relying upon and trusting God more and more.

The more you put your trust in God, the more you discover that He never lets you down. You can count on Him! When that happens, a boldness develops in your spirit so that anxiety is a thing of the past. You know who you are in Christ and who Christ is in you! You come to the place where you trust Him to be with you and to help you through whatever circumstances or experience life hands you.[11]

Dr. Stanley suggests that we ask four questions as we begin each day. Let me rephrase them here:

1. Am I trusting God today to provide for my needs? Read aloud these words from Philippians 4:19: "God…will supply all [my] needs from his glorious riches, which have been given to us in Christ Jesus."

2. Am I trusting God to be my security today? Read aloud these words from Job 24:23 NASB: "He provides them with security, and they are supported; and His eyes are on their ways."

3. Am I willing to risk some of what I have today because I am trusting God to meet my needs tomorrow? Read aloud these words from Psalm 23:1: "The LORD is my shepherd; I have everything I need."

4. Am I trusting God to show me his way? Read aloud these words from Psalm 32:8: "[Insert your name], 'I will guide

you along the best pathway for your life. I will advise you and watch over you.' "[12]

Rest for Our Souls

We're a leisure-oriented society, yet we're weary most of the time. If this weariness continues over a period of time, work suffers, the desire to continue diminishes, tempers flare, patience becomes non-existent, and soon we give up. We are tired all the time. And it's not a new problem. Over 50 years ago the author of *Springs in the Valley* shared this interesting tale from African colonial history:

> In the deep jungles of Africa a traveler was making a long trek. Coolies had been engaged from a tribe to carry the loads. The first day they marched rapidly and went far. The traveler had high hopes of a speedy journey. But the second morning these jungle tribesmen refused to move. For some reason they just sat and rested. On inquiry as to the reason for this strange behavior, the traveler was informed that they had gone too fast the first day and that *they were now waiting for their souls to catch up with their bodies.*

The author concludes with this penetrating exhortation: This whirling, rushing of life which so many of us live does for us what that first march did for those poor jungle tribesmen. The difference: *They knew* what was needed to restore life's balance; too often *we do not!*

Are your soul and body out of sync? Do you need to slow down so that your soul can catch up? What can you do to restore balance in your life? We can take comfort in knowing that God wants to help us with this process. Jesus says to each of us soul-weary people,

"Come to me, all of you who are weary and carry heavy burdens, and I will give you rest" (Matthew 11:28).

Let that invitation sink in for a minute. Jesus is asking you to come to him so that he can *give* you the rest you need. He didn't say, "Come to me, and I will tell you where you can find rest." He wants to *give* it to you. Other passages in Scripture remind us of the strength the Lord will give his children:

> You are my strength; I wait for you to rescue me, for you, O God, are my place of safety (Psalm 59:9).

> Have you never heard or understood? Don't you know that the LORD is the everlasting God, the Creator of all the earth? He never grows faint or weary. No one can measure the depths of his under-standing. He gives power to those who are tired and worn out; he offers strength to the weak. Even youths will become exhausted, and young men will give up. But those who wait on the LORD will find new strength. They will fly high on wings like eagles. They will run and not grow weary. They will walk and not faint (Isaiah 40:28-31).

> How precious is your unfailing love, O God!
> All humanity finds shelter in the shadow of your
>   wings.
> You feed them from the abundance of your own
>   house,
> letting them drink from your rivers of delight
> (Psalm 36:7-8).

We need rest for our souls. The psalmist says, "Those who live in the shelter of the Most High will find rest in the shadow of the Almighty. This I declare of the LORD: He alone is my refuge, my place of safety; he is my God, and I am trusting him" (Psalm 91:1-2).

Perhaps all that we have been pointing to in this book can be summed up in these words to a hymn by Ken Bible:

Lord, Life Becomes More Simple

Lord, life becomes more simple when all I seek is You,
When walking in Your Spirit is all that I pursue,
When knowing You are with me is all the light I need,
When all my heart is hungry for You to shape and lead.

Lord, life is filled with beauty when I am filled with You.
When You, so kind and patient, have made me caring, too.
When I am free to love You and look to You alone,
Then life has found its sunlight, and hope has found its home.

Lord Jesus, Sun of Heaven, its temple and its light,
Life's goal and its beginning, love's length and depth and height;
Lord, teach my heart to listen and rest in simple truth,
To know life's sweetest pleasure: to know and worship You.
I found life's sweetest pleasure: to know and worship You.[13]

Time for Reflection

1. What does rest mean to you?

2. Describe the times you feel rested.

3. What steps could you take to achieve a rhythm in your life?

4. What fear restricts you? How can the presence of Jesus in your life free you from this?

One Person's
Reflections on Life

🪶 *If my life were balanced, I would feel*…rested and at peace, as if my body and soul and emotions were in balance. I would feel as if time with God were as normal a part of my life as breathing.

🪶 *To me a fulfilled life means*…having a close relationship to God, letting him guide my decisions and activities.

🪶 *What keeps me from changing my life is*…my treadmill mentality. I need to keep in mind that if I am going to live life fully, I must slow down and use my mental, spiritual, and emotional energy wisely.

🪶 *If I were to have the life I always wanted, I would*…plan more time of quiet reflection, times that would charge my soul as well as my body. I would spend more quiet time with my family members.

14

Setting Up Our
Personal Plan

Well, you've read it all. You've finished this book. That's the first step. But where do you go from here? What will you do with what you have read? Will you file it and forget it? Will you remember it and use it?

In Chapter 1 you discovered that...

> Life isn't fulfilling—it's out of sync.
> Life isn't fulfilling—it's fragmented.
> Life isn't fulfilling—it's complicated.
> Life isn't fulfilling—it's stressful.
> Life isn't fulfilling—it's frantic.
> Life isn't fulfilling—it's overwhelming.

I hope that this scenario can soon become a distant memory as you replace it with the following:

> Life can be fulfilling—it's finding my rhythm.
> Life can be fulfilling—it's coming together.
> Life can be fulfilling—it's moving toward balance.
> Life can be fulfilling—it's more peaceful.
> Life can be fulfilling—it's relaxed.
> Life can be fulfilling—it's manageable.

Remember that a fulfilled life is a life of balance and faith. I'm assuming that your choice to read this chapter indicates that you're wanting to have the life you've always wanted. That's great. Now the work begins as you decide what you *want* to do, what you *will* do, and *how* you will do it.

At the end of chapter 1, you responded to four questions:

1. If my life were balanced, I would feel...

2. To me a fulfilling life means...

3. What keeps me from changing my life is...

4. If I were to have the life I wanted, I would...

Now that you have read this book as well as the responses other people have made to these four questions, how will you answer these questions now? Did your answers change? I hope that your goals and vision are a bit clearer from having asked the various questions posed throughout this book.

Where We've Been

Let's briefly review where we've been in this book. You were asked to identify the time bandits in your life. What did you discover? They could be anything from interruptions to procrastination, from fear of failure to failing to plan, from changing priorities to watching too much television. What decision have you made about the use of time in your life?

We discussed the hurry illness that has infected many people. Life to them is a rush. Their goal in life is to beat the clock and establish new speed records. This chapter encouraged you to develop a new sense of time. Numerous suggestions were given. Did you apply any, such as calling time-outs during the day, welcoming delays, or purposely slowing down?

Striving for success is a motivating factor for many people. After all, who wants to fail? You answered some important questions at the conclusion of chapter 4. In what area of your life would you like to be successful? Where would it benefit you and the kingdom of God for you to be successful? We may need to ask ourselves this question again and again throughout our lives.

We discussed the importance of living with balanced priorities. What does it mean to balance your life? Is urgency more a part of your life than balance? Instead of asking, "What do I have to do?" you might ask, "What do I choose to do today?" or "What would be best to do today?" or "What would glorify God the most in what I choose to do today?" This is key since a fulfilled life truly comes from glorifying him.

We talked about the problem of overloading our lives. We tend to do this because of disorganization, which can lead to the feeling of being out of control. How did you respond to the discussion on being a driven person? Did any of that hit home?

What did you discover about your energy drainers and energy boosters? Are you trying to be the "super" person? I hope you've been convinced to put away the cape. Did you identify your high and low energy times during the day? Making sure you have proper energy for what you are doing will make your life simpler.

I hope you caught the positive use of the word *downscaling*. Writing this book prompted me to downscale in several areas of my life. It's been a positive step. Have you decided how you will practice voluntary downscaling and simplicity? Did you complete the possessions inventory? If not, now would be a good time to return and to complete the process.

Have you been challenged to downscale your life by living on less? What is your present financial lifestyle? If you are not happy with it, what can you do to change it?

Do you have people who clutter your life? Most of us do. We all have some who are difficult to get along with and whom we can't avoid. For some it's an angry, explosive person, while others struggle along with a nonresponsive person. What steps have you taken to deal with the people who make your life unnecessarily complicated?

What did you discover about the excess baggage in your life? Many people are surprised to discover they have some. What have you done to lighten your load?

We discussed the importance of examining the clutter in our spiritual lives. Sometimes we end up doing things not because God has called us to do them but because we feel pressured or obligated to do them. Again, we need to find spiritual balance.

And we need to let our souls catch up to our bodies. That means planning times of leisure and rest for our bodies, our emotions, and our souls.

Drawing Up Your Plan

This chapter is critical because it brings you to the place of setting goals. You may love goals or hate them, but regardless, you need them—we all do. Goals focus our attention and action. They mobilize our energy and effort.

Take time now to write out your master plan. The plan is helpful because it will remind you where you want to go. Putting the plan into action may take many months, but setting your goals now will help you make sure that you are headed in the right direction.

My Plan to Discover
the Life I've Always Wanted

Step 1

I would like my life to be different in this way: _____

_____

_____

_____

_____

Step 2

A Scripture passage that I will memorize to help with the use of time in my life is: _____

_____

_____

_____

_____

Step 3

The time robber that I will change in my life is: __________

____

____

____

____

Step 4

I will take this step to inoculate myself against the hurry illness: ______________________________________

____

____

____

____

Step 5

I will look for my success in this way: ______________

____

____

____

____

I will balance my priorities, attitudes, and expectations by:

_____

_____

_____

_____

Step 6

The way in which I can glorify God is:_____

_____

_____

_____

_____

Step 7

I have identified as my area of overload: _____

_____

_____

_____

_____

To change this, I will: _____

_____

_____

_____

_____

Step 8

My greatest energy drainer is: _____

_____

_____

_____

What I will do to boost my energy is: _____

_____

_____

_____

_____

Step 9

To downscale my possessions, I will: _____

_____

_____

_____

_____

Step 10

To live on less, I will: _____

_____

_____

_____

Step 11

The people who clutter my life are: _____

_____

_____

_____

_____

I will take these steps to think about them differently: _____

_____

_____

_____

_____

This is how I will pray for them for the next month: _____

_____

_____

_____

_____

Step 12

My excess baggage is: _____

_____

_____

_____

_____

This is what I will do to lighten the baggage: _____

_____

_____

_____

_____

Step 13

To unclutter my spiritual life and achieve balance, I will:

_____

_____

_____

_____

Step 14

My plan to build times of leisure and rest into my life is:

_____

_____

_____

_____

Step 15

I'll review these goals in two-month intervals. These are the dates for review:

1._____

2._____

3._____

4._____

5._____

6._____

Step 16

My prayer for this process of discovering the life I've always wanted is: _____

_____

_____

_____

_____

Notes

Chapter 1—Getting the Life You Want

1. Richard A. Swenson, M.D., *Margin: How to Create the Emotional, Physical, Financial, and Time Reserves You Need* (Colorado Springs: NavPress, 1992), pp. 202-08, adapted. Used by permission.
2. Ibid., pp. 209-10.
3. Stephen R. Covey, A. Roger Merrill and Rebecca R. Merrill, *First Things First: A Principle-Centered Approach to Time and Life Management* (New York: Simon and Schuster, 1994), pp. 322-28.

Chapter 2—Time—Friend or Foe?

1. Richard D. Swenson, M.D., *Margin: How to Create the Emotional, Physical, Financial, and Time Reserves You Need* (Colorado Springs: NavPress, 1992), p. 147, adapted. Used by permission.
2. Quoted in Daniel J. Boorstin, *The Discoverers* (New York: Random House, 1983), p. 25.
3. Stephan Rechtschaffen, M.D., *Toward Time Freedom.*
4. Ann McGee-Cooper with Duane Trammell, *Time Management for Unmanageable People* (New York: Bantam Books, 1993), p. XVII, adapted.
5. Alec MacKenzie, *The Time Trap* (New York: American Management Association, 1990), p. 65, adapted.
6. Hyrum W. Smith, *The 10 Natural Laws of Successful Time and Life Management* (New York: Warner Books, 1994), pp. 28-34, adapted.

7. Jeff Davidson, *Complete Idiot's Guide to Managing Your Time* (New York: Simon & Schuster, 1995), p. 75, adapted.

8. Miriam Elliott, Ph.D., and Susan Meltsner, *The Perfectionist Predicament* (New York: William Morrow and Co., 1991), pp. 106-11, adapted.

9. Smith, *The 10 Natural Laws,* pp. 28-36, adapted.

10. Davidson, *Complete Idiot's Guide,* p. 19, adapted.

11. Ibid., pp. 18-21.

12. Don Aslett, *How to Have a 48-Hour Day* (Cincinnati: Better Books, 1996), p. 39, adapted.

13. Tim Hansel, *When I Relax, I Feel Guilty* (Elgin, IL: Chariot Victor Books, 1979), p. 69, adapted. Used by permission.

14. Leslie Flynn, *It's About Time* (Newtown, PA: Timothy Books, 1974), p. 24, adapted.

15. Michel Quoist, *Prayers* (Dublin: M.H. Gill, 1965), pp. 76-78.

16. Rechtschaffen, M.D., p. 13, adapted.

17. Hansel, *When I Relax,* p. 71, adapted.

18. Ken Gire, *Windows of the Soul* (Grand Rapids, MI: Zondervan, 1996), pp. 34-36, adapted.

Chapter 3—The Hurry Illness

1. Ralph Keyes, *Timelock* (New York: HarperCollins, 1991), p. 9, adapted.

2. Ann McGee-Cooper with Duane Trammell, *Time Management for Unmanageable People* (New York: Bantam Books, 1993), pp. 14-15, adapted.

3. Marshall Cook, *Slow Down and Get More Done* (Cincinnati: Betterway Books, 1993), p. 95, adapted.

4. Stephan Rechtschaffen, M.D., *Toward Time Freedom.*

5. Bob Welch, *More to Life Than Having It All* (Eugene, OR: Harvest House, 1991), pp. 36-37. Used by permission.

6. Patrick Morley, *Seven Seasons of a Man's Life* (Grand Rapids, MI: Zondervan, 1997), p. 25. Used by permission

7. Nikos Kazantzakis, *Zorba the Greek* (New York: Ballantine Books, 1952), pp. 138-39. Used by permission.

8. Charles R. Swindoll, *Strike the Original Match* (Portland, OR: Multnomah Press, 1980), p. 92. Used by permission.

9. Keyes, *Timelock,* pp. 214-19.

10. Tim Hansel, *When I Relax, I Feel Guilty* (Elgin, IL: Chariot Victor Books, 1979), p. 55. Used by permission.

Chapter 4—How Do We Measure Success?

1. Quoted in Gary Rosberg, *Guard Your Heart* (Portland, OR: Multnomah, 1994), pp. 134-35. Used by permission.

2. Steve Farrar, *If I'm Not Tarzan, And My Wife Isn't Jane, Then What Are We Doing in the Jungle?* (Portland, OR: Multnomah Press, 1991), pp. 65-66, adapted.

3. Bruce Shelley, *The Gospel of the American Dream* (Portland, OR: Multnomah Press, 1989), p. 133. Used by permission

4. Farrar, *If I'm Not Tarzan,* pp. 65-66, adapted.

5. Gary Aumiller, *Keeping It Simple: Sorting Out What Really Matters in Your Life* (Holbrook, MA: Adams Media Corp., 1995), p. vi, (adapted and updated). Used by permission.

6. Archibald Hart, *15 Principles for Achieving Happiness* (Dallas: Word, 1988), pp. 33-34.

7. Ron Jenson, *Make a Life, Not Just a Living* (Nashville: Thomas Nelson, 1995), pp. XXIII-XXV, adapted.

8. Carole Hyatt and Linda Gottlieb, *When Smart People Fail* (New York: Simon & Schuster, 1987), pp. 206-08, adapted.

9. Terry Hershey, *Young Adult Ministry* (Loveland, CO: Group Publishing, 1986), p. 39. Used by permission.

10. "Pilot of the Airwaves," *Dallas Morning News,* Oct. 7, 1990, "Today Section," p. 1, adapted.

11. Gary Paulsen, "The Last Great Race," *Reader's Digest,* March 1994, and Gary Paulsen, *Winterdance* (Orlando: Harcourt, Brace & Co., 1994), pp. 299, 301, adapted.

12. Wallace Terry, "When His Sound Was Silenced," *Parade Magazine,* December 25, 1994, pp. 12-13, adapted.

13. Gary J. Oliver, *How to Get It Right After You've Gotten It Wrong* (Wheaton, IL: Victor Books, 1995), pp. 166-73, adapted. Used by permission.

14. Ibid., p. 27.

15. Ibid., p. 17.

16. Rosberg, *Guard Your Heart,* pp. 138-39.

17. Rick Warren, *The Purpose-Driven Life* (Grand Rapids, MI: Zondervan, 2003), p. 249.

18. Patrick Morley, *Seven Seasons of a Man's Life* (Grand Rapids, MI: Zondervan, 1997), pp. 151-56. Used by permission.

Chapter 5—Living with Balanced Priorities

1. Linda Eyre and Richard Eyre, *Lifebalance* (New York: Ballantine Books, 1987), p. 16. Used by permission.

2. Charles Hummel, *Tyranny of the Urgent* (Downers Grove, IL: InterVarsity Press, 1967), pp. 9-10. Used by permission.

3. Stephen R. Covey, A. Roger Merrill, and Rebecca R. Merrill, *First Things First: A Principle-Centered Approach to Time and Life Management* (New York: Simon & Schuster, 1994), pp. 88-89, adapted.

4. Eyre and Eyre, *Lifebalance,* pp. 14-16.

5. Michael LeBoeuf, *Working Smart: How to Accomplish More in Half the Time* (New York: McGraw-Hill, 1979), pp. 52-53, adapted.

6. Covey, Merrill, and Merrill, *First Things First,* pp. 169, 184.

7. Miriam Elliott and Susan Meltsner, *The Perfectionist Predicament: How to Curb Your Expectations and Learn to Live with Foibles, Flaws and Failings in the Real World* (New York: William Morrow, 1991), pp. 216-22, adapted.

Chapter 6—Overloaded and Driven

1. Alec Mackenzie, *The Time Trap* (New York: American Management Association, 1990), p. 90.

2. Gordon MacDonald, *Ordering Your Private World* (Nashville: Thomas Nelson, 1984), pp. 64-67. Used by permission.

3. Hyrum W. Smith, *The 10 Natural Laws of Successful Time and Life Management* (New York: Warner Books, 1994), p. 21.

4. Ibid.

5. Linda Eyre and Richard Eyre, *Lifebalance* (New York: Ballantine Books, 1987), p. 101. Used by permission.

6. Charles Stanley, *The Source of My Strength* (Nashville: Thomas Nelson, 1994), pp. 189-91. Used by permission.

7. MacDonald, *Ordering Your Private World,* p. 34.

8. Ibid., pp. 31-36.

9. Max Lucado, *In the Eye of a Storm* (Dallas: Word, 1994), pp. 97-98.

10. Ann McGee-Cooper, *You Don't Have to Go Home from Work Exhausted* (New York: Bantam Books, 1990), p. 53.

11. Rick Warren, *The Purpose-Driven Life* (Grand Rapids, MI: Zondervan, 2003), p. 63.

Chapter 7—Energy Drainers and Energy Boosters

1. Michael LeBoeuf, *Working Smart: How to Accomplish More in Half the Time* (New York: Warner Books, 1979), pp. 23-35, adapted.

2. Ann McGee-Cooper, *You Don't Have to Go Home from Work Exhausted* (New York: Bantam Books, 1990), pp. 150-58.

3. Ibid., pp. 18-32.

4. Stephen R. Covey, *The Seven Habits of Highly Effective People* (New York: Simon & Schuster, 1989), pp. 71-72, adapted.

5. McGee-Cooper, *You Don't Have to Go Home,* pp. 61-82, adapted.

Chapter 8—Downscaling Our Things

1. Lee Smith, "Burned-Out Bosses," *Fortune,* July 25, 1994, pp. 44-46, adapted.

2. Amy Saltzman, *Downshifting: Reinventing Success on a Slower Track* (New York: Harper Perennial, 1992), pp. 17-18.

3. Tim Kimmel, *Surviving Life in the Fast Lane* (Colorado Springs: NavPress, 1990), p. 62. Used by permission.

4. Howard Dayton, Jr., *Your Money: Frustration or Freedom?* (Wheaton, IL: Tyndale House, 1979), p. 39. Used by permission.

5. Gary S. Aumiller, *Keeping It Simple: Sorting Out What Really Matters in Your Life* (Holbrook, MA: Adams Media Corp., 1995), pp. 17-21. Used by permission.

6. Dave and Kathy Babbitt, *Downscaling* (Chicago: Moody Press, 1993), p. 119. Used by permission.

7. Michael LeBoeuf, *Working Smart: How to Accomplish More in Half the Time* (New York: Warner Books, 1979), pp. 55-56.

8. Barbara DeGrote-Sorenson and David Allen Sorenson, *'Tis a Gift to Be Simple* (Minneapolis: Augsburg Fortress, 1992), p. 24. Used by permission.

9. Ibid., p. 16.

10. Ibid.

11. Aumiller, *Keeping It Simple,* pp. 27-31.

12. LeBoeuf, *Working Smart,* p. 99.

Chapter 9—Living on Less

1. Linda Eyre and Richard Eyre, *Lifebalance* (New York: Ballantine Books, 1987), p. 72, adapted.

2. Patrick Morley, *The Seven Seasons of a Man's Life* (Grand Rapids, MI: Zondervan, 1997), pp. 90-91, adapted. Used by permission.

3. Karen O'Connor, *When Spending Takes the Place of Feeling* (Nashville: Thomas Nelson, 1992), p. 87, adapted.

4. Dave and Kathy Babbitt, *Downscaling* (Chicago: Moody Press, 1993), pp. 149-50. Used by permission.

Chapter 10—The People Who Clutter Our Lives

1. Les Parrott III, *High-Maintenance Relationships* (Wheaton, IL: Tyndale House, 1996), p. 47.

2. Miriam Elliott and Susan Meltsner, *The Perfectionist Predicament: How to Curb Your Expectations and Learn to Live with Foibles, Flaws and Failings in the Real World* (New York: William Morrow, 1991), pp. 264-67, adapted.

3. Steven J. Hendlin, *When Good Enough Is Never Enough* (New York: G.P. Putnam's Sons, 1992), adapted, pp. 205-10.

4. H. Norman Wright and Gary J. Oliver, *How to Bring Out the Best in Your Spouse* (Ann Arbor, MI: Servant, 1996), pp. 201-19.

5. For help in this area, read *Type Talk* by Otto Kroeger and Janet Thuesen (New York: Dell, 1989).

Chapter 11—Dumping Excess Emotional Baggage
1. David Viscott, *Risking* (New York: Pocket Book, 1977), pp. 8-21, 28, adapted.
2. Judith Sills, *Excess Baggage* (New York: Penguin Books, 1993), pp. 30-71, adapted.; Sandra Hirsh and Jean Kummerow, *Life Types* (New York: Warner Books, 1989), pp. 52-63, adapted.

Chapter 12—Doing the Best Thing
1. Gordon MacDonald, *Restoring Your Spiritual Passion* (Nashville: Thomas Nelson, 1986), p. 30.
2. Ibid., p. 43.
3. Charles Stanley, *The Source of My Strength* (Nashville: Thomas Nelson, 1994), p. 199. Used by permission.
4. Ibid., p. 196.
5. Malcolm Smith, *Spiritual Burnout* (Tulsa, OK: Honor Books, 1988), p. 169.
6. David Stoop, *Seeking God Together* (Wheaton, IL: Tyndale House, 1996), pp. 91-92. Words and music to the chorus by Rodney Johnson © 1995 Refreshing Music/BMI, Adm. by Integrated Music, Inc.
7. Richard Foster, *The Celebration of Discipline* (San Francisco: Harper & Row, 1988), pp. 95-96.
8. J.I. Packer, *Knowing God* (Downers Grove, IL: InterVarsity Press, 1973), p. 37.
9. "And the Father Will Dance." Arranged by Mark Hayes, lyrics adapted from Zephaniah 3:14,17 and Psalm 54:2,4. Used by permission.
10. John Piper, *The Pleasures of God* (Portland, OR: Multnomah, 1991), p. 188.
11. Stoop, *Seeking God Together,* pp. 112-13.
12. Foster, *Celebration of Discipline,* pp. 128-30.
13. Ibid., pp. 295-300.

Chapter 13—Letting Our Souls Catch Up to Our Bodies
1. Gordon Dahl, *Work, Play and Worship in a Leisure-Oriented Society* (Minneapolis: Augsburg, 1972), p. 12. Used by permission.
2. Joe B. Brown, *Battle Fatigue* (Nashville: Broadman and Holman, 1995), pp. 13-14.
3. Amy Saltzman, *Downshifting: Reinventing Success on a Slower Track* (New York: HarperPerennial, 1991), pp. 203-10, adapted.
4. Tim Hansel, *When I Relax, I Feel Guilty* (Elgin, IL: Chariot Victor Books, 1979), pp. 29-30. Used by permission.
5. Ibid., pp. 30-31.
6. Richard A. Swenson, M.D., *Margin: How to Create Emotional, Physical, Financial, and Time Reserves You Need* (Colorado Springs: 1992), p. 230, adapted. Used by permission.

7. Richard Foster, *The Freedom of Simplicity* (San Francisco: Harper & Row, 1981), p. 91.

8. Richard Exley, *The Rhythm of Life* (Tulsa, OK: Honor Books, 1982), p. 77, adapted. Used by permission.

9. David L. McKenna, *The Communicator's Commentary* (Dallas, TX: Word, 1982), p. 77.

10. Exley, *Rhythm,* p. 83.

11. Charles Stanley, *The Source of My Strength* (Nashville: Thomas Nelson, 1994), pp. 36-37. Used by permission.

12. Ibid., pp. 45-54.

13. Words by Ken Bible, "Lord, Life Becomes More Simple" (Nashville: Pilot Point Music, 1994). Integrated Copyright Group, Inc., P.O. Box 24149, Nashville, TN 37202), song 1173681. Used by permission.

More Books by

H. Norman Wright

Relationship Books

101 Questions to Ask Before You Get Engaged

After You Say "I Do"

After You Say "I Do" Devotional

Before You Remarry

Before You Say "I Do"®

Before You Say "I Do"® Devotional

Finding Your Perfect Mate

Helping Your Kids Deal with Anger, Fear, and Sadness

Quiet Times for Couples

Quiet Times for Those Who Need Comfort

Winning Over Your Emotions

Gift Books

Everything I Know About Parenting I
Learned from My Puppy

A Friend Like No Other

My Dog Changed My Life

Other Great Books from
Harvest House

A WOMAN AFTER GOD'S OWN HEART®
Elizabeth George

With more than 735,000 copies sold, *A Woman After God's Own Heart* has reached women in all walks of life and circumstances, encouraging them to follow God. Offering gentle advice, spiritual wisdom, and practical applications, Elizabeth shares how you can seek God's heart in every area of your life. You'll discover peace and purpose as you prepare your heart and mind to embrace God's plan every day.

A MAN AFTER GOD'S OWN HEART
Jim George

Do you want to be a man after God's own heart...but wonder how to become one? Author Jim George shows that a heartfelt desire to grow spiritually is all you need. God's grace does the rest—bringing lasting change to a man's marriage, work, and witness. Realize the tremendous joy and confidence that comes from pursuing God in every area of your life!

THE PRAYER THAT CHANGES EVERYTHING®
Stormie Omartian

Stormie's passion for communing with the Lord shines through as she encourages you to develop an attitude—an attitude of praise, worship, and thanksgiving to God—and to live each day making praise your first reaction and not a last resort. In *The Prayer That Changes Everything* you'll find Stormie's personal stories, biblical truths, and practical guiding principles that reveal the wonders that take place when we offer praise in the middle of difficulties, sorrow, fear, and, yes, abundance and joy.

THE DAILY BIBLE®
F. LaGard Smith

This unique chronological presentation of God's story in the New International Version reveals God's heart in daily readings. You'll also discover the historical progression of the books of the Bible, devotional commentary, and topical arrangement of Proverbs and Ecclesiastes.

THE GOOD HUSBAND'S GUIDE TO BALANCING HOBBIES & MARRIAGE
Steve Chapman

Avid hunter Steve Chapman enthusiastically pursues a lifelong hobby while remaining passionate about his wife and home. His nine life-changing principles to balancing hobbies and marriage—including investing equal finances in his spouse's interests, spending more time with his wife than his hobby, and sharing the child-rearing load—will help every sportsman.

WHEN YOUR PAST IS HURTING YOUR PRESENT
Sue Augustine

Are you struggling with a difficult past? Is your past harming your present life and crippling your future? With compassion and empathy—and plenty of "telling on herself" humor—author Sue Augustine shows you how to understand and break patterns that might be holding you back from God's best, including overcoming a victim mentality, identifying, releasing, and changing your view of the past, and settings goals for the future with confidence.

THE HEALING POWER OF FORGIVENESS
Ray Pritchard

Why is forgiveness so difficult? Must we forgive when it's the other person's fault? What if we feel we can't forgive because we've been hurt so badly? When we hold grudges, seek retribution, and blame others, we short-circuit our ability to live the Christian life the way it's meant to be lived. Ray Pritchard shows you how to find freedom, peace, and emotional healing.

HARVEST HOUSE
PUBLISHERS